Pastor David's Travel Guide to

HEAVEN

Shagufta,

God has prepared
a place for you!

John 14:2

D O Dykes

DAVID O. DYKES

FLUENCY
TELLING STORIES THAT MATTER

Produced with the assistance of Fluency Organization, Inc.
Graphic design: Inkwell Creative

If God hath made this world so fair,
Where sin and death abound;
How beautiful beyond compare
Will Paradise be found!

–From "The Earth Full of the Goodness of God"
James Montgomery, 1771–1854

INTRODUCTION

A couple of years ago I traveled with my daughter, son-in-law, and their three kids to Disney World. Like true millennials, they utilized a travel app on their smartphones that displayed real-time data on the wait time at each attraction. The app even used algorithms to suggest the ideal attraction or ride to visit at any given moment.

I smiled as I remembered how I had once led my family through Disney World a couple of decades earlier when brick cell phones were amazing and travel apps were the stuff of science fiction. Ever the planner, I had depended then on my paperback copy of *Rick Steves' Travel Guide to Disney World*. With this trusty guide firmly in hand, I knew the optimum time to arrive and precisely where to line up when the park opened. He even gave instructions on the order to see each of the attractions.

I got to thinking that I'd like to write a travel guide to the ultimate pleasure destination: Heaven. Whenever you plan a trip to visit a new city or even a new country, it's best to have an insider—a local resident—guide you as you plan your trip. When it comes to Heaven, I'm not the insider. Jesus is. He resides in Heaven and gives us ample information in His book for us to learn about His Home Country. Drawing on several decades of studying the Bible and preaching, I put together *Pastor David's Travel Guide to Heaven*. It's based on what the Bible says about Heaven to give interested travelers as much information as they need to enjoy a pleasant trip one day to what could be their eternal home.

Heaven is the ultimate destination for every person who has ever trusted Jesus Christ as Lord and Savior. If that's true for you, you're relocating there one day to spend all of eternity—so don't you think it's worthwhile to see what the Bible has to say about it?

PART 1

PLANNING THE TRIP OF A LIFETIME

CHAPTER 1

THE HISTORY OF HEAVEN

"Heaven is more wonderful than you can ever imagine."

With those words, my mother launched me as a young child on a quest to find out as much as I could about this place called Heaven. And I am still learning about it every day. Heaven first became real to me around age six when my grandfather died unexpectedly. My mother tried to comfort me that night after dinner by explaining that he was now in Heaven. I remember I had a lot of questions about what that meant. *Where was that? What was it like? What was he doing now?* I wanted to know all the details about where my grandfather was.

My mother was a devoted believer, but I remember she didn't have a lot of detailed answers. I'm sure she grew annoyed by my peppering her with questions while she was trying to finish the dishes. She finally smiled at me, took a deep breath, and just said, "David, Heaven is more wonderful that you can ever imagine." I went to bed that night intrigued. If Heaven was better than anything I could imagine, then that had to be something. I've always had a very active imagination that landed me in a lot of trouble when I was a young kid because I often got lost in the plot of the adventure books that I read under the covers by flashlight way after bedtime. There was no way I could sleep that night because I was too busy trying to picture what Heaven was like.

40 Things You WON'T Find in Heaven

① Police Officers

I knew a little about Heaven because my family always attended church where we sang wonderful songs like "When We All Get to Heaven." As I grew older and many of my loved ones who knew the Lord died and went to Heaven, I longed to know even more about this destination. It was as if they had departed on a journey to a mysterious and far-off place and I wanted to understand exactly where they'd gone.

What do you think Heaven is like?

According to a 2013 Pew Research poll 74% of Americans believe in Heaven, and 54% believe that if they do enough good deeds, they can earn entrance into Heaven after they die. Interestingly, only 39% of Americans believe in hell. Based on my experience as a pastor, I think these stats are accurate because even among Christians there is widespread ignorance about the biblical details of Heaven.

If you ask a Christian what Heaven will be like they'll often give short answers like, "beautiful" or "wonderful" or "paradise." Let's imagine that you are planning an expensive two-week vacation to Costa Rica. The easiest thing to do is use a travel agent and let them plan the trip for you. But most of us want to do some of our own research online. So you go online to learn everything you can about Costa Rica. But when you Google Costa Rica there are only three words on the website: "Beautiful, Wonderful, Paradise." You wouldn't be satisfied. You'd want to know MORE! You'd want to know the history, the climate, the language, the currency, the places to eat, and the places to stay.

Many people think that Heaven is going to be some kind of spooky ethereal place where we're going to be floating around on soft white clouds playing harps. But the first thing to understand about Heaven is that it's a REAL place. In fact I capitalize the word *Heaven*, just as I would capitalize the cities of London or Paris. It's a proper noun.

God is the architect and builder of Heaven

If you could describe what you've heard Heaven is like in one word, what would it be? Mysterious? Unknown? If so, I'm glad you're reading this book because the Bible actually has a lot to say about Heaven. The word *Heaven* appears more than 600 times in the Bible. In the Old Testament the Hebrew word for Heaven is *shamayim* (Heavens). In the New Testament the Greek word is *ouranos*. It makes sense that God had a lot to say about Heaven because He wants us to spend eternity there with Him.

First, the Bible says that God is the architect and builder of Heaven. In every city on the planet there are roads and buildings. Each of these was designed by an architect and built by a construction company. The same is true of Heaven, but Heaven is unlike any earthly city because God Himself is both the architect and builder.

Every earthly city that stands today is built on a foundation made by human hands, which means it will one day collapse and crumble like all of the civilizations prior have done. I have visited the Tel Megiddo in Israel dozens of times. At this ancient site 26 different layers of civilizations have been built and destroyed one on top of the other like layers in a cake. But God laid the foundation for the city of Heaven, and it will never crumble. It will stand for all eternity!

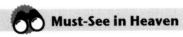 **Must-See in Heaven**

People of every race, nation, tribe, and language

"After this I looked, and there was a vast multitude from every nation, tribe, people, and language, which no one could number, standing before the throne and before the Lamb. They were clothed in white robes with palm branches in their hands." — **REVELATION 7:9** (csb)

The people make Heaven a great place

The Bible talks about Heaven as both a city and a country. It's a real place because it's a real city. But when I think of a country, I think about the people who live there. The writer of Hebrews in the New Testament doesn't just confirm that Heaven is a country, he describes it as a BETTER COUNTRY. I was born in Alabama but I got to Texas as quickly as I could. Texans believe that they are the best state in the Union because of their people. In the same way, the writer of Hebrews is saying that Heaven is a better country because of the residents there. I'll be writing much more about the residents of this Better Country, but for now let's take a sneak peek at them.

In Hebrews 11 we meet a group of people who are already in Heaven. Pastors often call this list the "Roll Call of Faith" because it contains the names and faithful deeds of many of the heroes of the Bible. When you read this list, you quickly discover that they all had one thing in common besides their great faith. They were all looking forward to a better country—a Heavenly country.

40 Things You WON'T Find in Heaven

(2) War

Consider Abraham. God promised him that he would have so many descendants that they would be like the stars in the sky. God called him to leave where he was and follow him to a new land he knew nothing about.

Hebrews 11:8-11 says, *"By faith Abraham, when called to go to a place he would later receive as his inheritance, obeyed and went, even though he did not know where he was going. By faith he made his home in the promised land like a stranger in a foreign country; he lived in tents, as did Isaac and Jacob, who were heirs with him of the same promise. For he was looking forward to the city with foundations, whose architect and builder is God. And by faith even Sarah, who was past childbearing age, was enabled to bear children because she considered him faithful who had made the promise."*

Abraham looked past this great promise to something else far off in a Heavenly future. The Bible says he wasn't focused on his new address somewhere in the Middle East—he squinted and looked right past that in anticipation of living in a city built by God. He was looking forward to Heaven.

Hebrews 11:13-16 says, *"All these people were still living by faith when they died. They did*

> **Travel Tips**
>
> ■ For a tasty treat, try the fruit produced by the Tree of Life. It's always in season!

not receive the things promised; they only saw them and welcomed them from a distance, admitting that they were foreigners and strangers on earth. People who say such things show that they are looking for a country of their own. If they had been thinking of the country they had left, they would have had opportunity to return. Instead, they were longing for a BETTER country—a heavenly one. Therefore God is not ashamed to be called their God, for he has prepared a city for them."

Abraham and all these great saints were preoccupied with this Heavenly city and BETTER COUNTRY throughout their lifetime. We're the exact opposite, truth be told. We have a lot more time and energy invested into the city and country where we live now, wherever that may be. We drive the roads. We shop the malls. We walk the neighborhoods. We'll all live here 70, 80, maybe 90 years at best—but I want to get you thinking about what the Bible constantly reminds us to think about—what's coming next. Where will you spend all of eternity long after your time on earth is over?

The history of Heaven

Every city and country on earth has a recorded history. What about Heaven? The history of Heaven is intertwined with the history of God. And God lives above the timeline of human history. He has always existed, so the same can be said of

Heaven. The Bible tells us, *"From everlasting to everlasting you are God"* (Psalm 90:2). It's difficult for our feeble minds to grasp the truth that God transcends both time and space.

In the part of Texas where I live it's not unusual to drive past a historical marker outside nearby cities and towns. These plaques usually tell the story of the first settlers or key individuals responsible for building the city. They also have a built-in inexplicable attraction for fathers. Many a family has pulled over on a drive to let Dad get out and read the historical marker, not to mention pose for a picture beside it.

The first verse in the Bible states that there was a time, in the beginning, when God created the Heavens (plural) and the earth (singular). If Heaven had a historical marker outside its gates it might read something like this:

HEAVEN
BACK BEFORE TIME BEGAN,
GOD CREATED THIS CITY...

A good starting place to learn about Heaven is to understand that the Bible uses Heaven to describe three different spheres of existence. There's a popular expression about being in "seventh Heaven," but according to the Bible there aren't seven Heavens. You might be surprised to learn that the tradition of seven Heavens comes from the teachings of Islam.

Travel Preview

⭐⭐⭐⭐⭐

Every challenge, hardship, and worry will pale in comparison to Heaven's bright light of Jesus. Oh, the relief.

CATHY C.

Three Heavens in the Bible

First, Heaven is used to describe the atmosphere around the earth—what we call "the air." In Genesis 1:20 God said, *"let birds fly above the earth in the open expanse of the heavens" (ESV).*

Second, Heaven is used to describe what we would call outer space where God created the moon and stars. The Bible says in Psalm 8:3, *"When I consider the heavens, the work of your fingers, the moon and the stars, which you have set in place."*

40 Things You WON'T Find in Heaven

③ Guns

The third description of Heaven, and the one we're going to be focusing on in this travel guide, is the dwelling place of God. Daniel said to King Nebuchadnezzar, *"There is a God in heaven who reveals mysteries"* (Daniel 2:28).

Think of the difference between the three Heavens this way. You can see the first Heaven (the sky) by DAY. You see the second Heaven (the stars) by NIGHT. And you see the third Heaven by FAITH.

In 2 Corinthians 12, Paul refers to a man in Christ who had a vision of being caught up to this third Heaven where God lives. Most scholars suggest that this was New Testament writer the apostle Paul himself but modesty prevented him from bragging about it. Paul described this third Heaven as "paradise." The word *paradise* comes from a Persian word that means "beautiful garden."

Paradise is found only two other times in the New Testament—both times by Jesus. In his dying moments Jesus said to the thief beside him on the cross, *"Today you will be with me in paradise"* (Luke 23:43). And in the letter that the resurrected and glorified Christ wrote to the church at Ephesus He says, *"To him who overcomes I will give the right to eat from the tree of life which is in the paradise of God"* (Revelation 2:7).

I love that the narrative of the Bible begins with a garden and ends with a garden. Genesis opens with God creating the Garden of Eden and enjoying fellowship with two people in Paradise. The Bible concludes with the last book of the Bible in Revelation with God enjoying fellowship with a multitude of people in a Heavenly garden called Paradise.

Paradise, the third Heaven where God lives, is a real place. There are many other ways that Heaven is described, but in every case we're told that God built it. For example, in 2 Corinthians 5:1 we read, *"Now we know that if the earthly tent we live in is destroyed, we have a building from God, an eternal house in heaven, not built by human hands."* It's imperative that we understand that Heaven is not a place of our own making—it's the creation of God alone. Clearly He wants us to know He alone is behind the idea.

This "building" in 2 Corinthians is not referring to a structure of wood or masonry. The context of this passage tells us that it's referring to the eternal physical body that we'll be given in Heaven. We'll go deeper into this truth in later chapters, and I guarantee that you will learn some things about Heaven that you never knew before! But at this point let's continue our focus on the fact that nothing is built by human hands in Heaven.

God-created or manmade?

Many years ago we decided to build a new home in Alabama. Pastors don't necessarily have a lot of building skills, myself included. However, one of my friends owned a building supply store, and there were other members of the church who had different construction skills. We were on a tight budget so rather than spend the money to contract with an experienced homebuilder, we decided to undertake the project ourselves and invest a lot of "sweat equity" in it.

First we bought a vacant lot and hired a local architect to design a small house that we could afford. Then we took the plans to a bank for a loan. This was in the early 1980s, so we were happy to get a construction loan at a rate somewhere

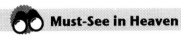 **Must-See in Heaven**

The Crystal Glass Sea in Front of God's Throne

"Something like a sea of glass, similar to crystal, was also before the throne. Four living creatures covered with eyes in front and in back were around the throne on each side."

— REVELATION 4:6 (csb)

around 14% interest! Next we hired someone to clear the lot, dig the foundation, and pour the concrete footings. I became the assistant in all these jobs and learned a lot from the men who did each job. After the house was framed and "in the dry," I pulled all the electrical wire and installed the boxes for the light fixtures and plugs. Since my day job was a full-time pastor, I worked on our home at night and every Saturday. After about four months of backbreaking work the house was finally completed. To me, it was a masterpiece! We were so proud. We had a moving-in celebration and invited all the different workers to join us as we dedicated the house to God.

Soon after moving in, I noticed that some things that weren't exactly as perfect as they seemed on dedication day. Some of the rooms were too small for their intended use. I discovered that I had wired a three-way electrical switch wrong, and it blew a fuse when I tried to turn a light on one day. There was a growing list of several other things that we needed to fix. A few years ago I drove to Alabama and went by our old house. It seemed so tiny and in desperate need of repair! One thing I learned through that experience is that any house "built with human hands" will always be FAR from perfect.

40 Things You WON'T Find in Heaven

④ Pharmacies

But when the Master Architect and Builder designs and builds something, it is eternal and perfect. Everything works as intended and it stands for eternity! Heaven is as old as time itself, but it will remain as new as the first day God created it a trillion centuries after our sun has cooled and the stars have all been plucked from the sky. Heaven is both faultless and timeless.

Faith in Heaven

If Heaven is a real city, it has its own economy—including a currency. Let's find out about the currency of Heaven and what all it can secure for you in this life—and in the life to come.

Travel Preview

★★★★★

Heaven will be where we see Jesus face to face and say thank you...We can get the answers to all our questions and be reunited with the ones we love.

JAN H.

CHAPTER 2

THE CURRENCY OF HEAVEN

When you visit a foreign country you want to know what currency they use, and you need to exchange your currency if you are going to make purchases. When I travel to the Philippines I convert U.S. dollars to Filipino pesos. When I travel to France, I exchange dollars for euros. There are some countries around the world that accept dollars, but most countries only accept their national currency. For instance, when you're in England, don't try using dollars. They only accept pounds sterling.

In Heaven there is only one currency that is accepted, and it is the currency of faith. And this currency is the STRONGEST in the universe and it holds its value forevermore! The Bible says, *"And without faith it is impossible to please God, because anyone who comes to God must believe that he exists and that he rewards those who earnestly seek him"* (Hebrews 11:6).

In the mid-1990s our church had partnered with several Russian Baptist churches in the Crimea. This was the time after the fall of the Iron Curtain and the value of Russian ruble had tumbled to an all-time low. One American dollar was worth 5,000 Russian rubles. Can you imagine? Your dollar would have 5,000 times more purchasing power at a Russian dollar store (if there had been such a thing). When the local pastor there helped us exchange our U.S. dollars at a Russian bank, the tellers gave us large grocery bags full of Russian money. I recall one evening when it cost 300,000 rubles to fill up Pastor Benjamin's van with gasoline!

The wonderful thing about Heaven's currency is that you don't have to have bags full of faith to please God. Even a little bit of faith is extremely valuable. Jesus said that faith the size of a mustard seed can move an entire mountain. It's not the size of or the amount of faith that has spiritual purchasing power—it's the OBJECT of our faith that gives it value. In other words, who or what you invest your faith in is what matters.

Some people say they don't have any faith at all—they're not religious, they claim. I've observed that everyone displays faith constantly throughout their everyday activities. Whenever we drive over a bridge, we put faith in that the bridge will hold the weight of the car. When we sit on a chair, we put faith in the chair to support our body. When we take medicine, we place faith in the doctor who prescribed it, the pharmacist who filled it, and the manufacturer who made it.

The value of Heaven's currency is found in the object of our faith—a living God who loves us so much and wants the very best for us. When was the last time you came to God with the tiniest bit of faith that you could muster and asked Him to move a mountain? Jesus says we can do that. Oh, you haven't done that lately because you're looking at the size of the mountain? It looks too big and scary, you say? Read on.

Travel Preview

★★★★★

Heaven is free of heartache and sickness. All is peaceful and serene. My whole family will be united again, never more to part. But the most beautiful thing is being in the presence of God Almighty!

FELICIA M.

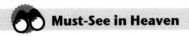 **Must-See in Heaven**

The Lamb's Book of Life

"Nothing unclean will ever enter it, nor anyone who does what is detestable or false, but only those written in the Lamb's book of life."
— REVELATION 21:27 (csb)

What does faith cost?

So if faith is Heaven's currency, what is it that we must exchange for this currency? We must exchange SIGHT. The Bible says, *"We live by faith; not by sight"* (2 Corinthians 5:7). We have five physical senses: seeing, hearing, feeling, smelling, touching. Of these, sight is the major sense. For all Heavenly transactions we must be willing to exchange living by our five senses for living by faith. Sight says, "Give me proof of Heaven and I'll believe." Faith says, "I'll believe without any proof."

I once read about an agnostic college professor who was trying to convince his students that God didn't exist. He said to them, "Look out the classroom window. Do you see the buildings?" They all nodded. "Do you see the trees?" They nodded in agreement again. "Do you see the grass?" Once more, they nodded. "Do you see the clouds?" Again they nodded in affirmation. Then he said, "Do you see God?" They shook their heads no. The professor then summarized, "Exactly. Buildings, trees, grass, and clouds exist. But God does not exist."

Just when the professor was feeling smug about his logic, a Christian student said, "Excuse me, sir. May I ask the class some questions?" He said, "Sure." She turned to her classmates and said, "Look at the professor. Do you see his hair?" They nodded. "Do you see his face?" They nodded. "Do you see his shirt?" Again they nodded, unsure where she was going. Then she said, "Do you see his brain?" They snickered and shook their heads no. She said, "Using the same logic, then we know that our professor's brain doesn't exist!"

Remember, the great saints listed in the Roll Call of Faith in Hebrews 11 died without seeing Heaven, but they died believing they *would* see Heaven. They saw Heaven with eyes of faith and died with the full assurance that they would enter the

Travel Tips

■ To arrive safely in Heaven, be sure that you don't go down the wide road that leads to destruction. (Matthew 7:13-14)

city that God had prepared for them. If you have lost loved ones who put their faith in Christ as Savior and Lord, they died without seeing Heaven. But by faith they died believing that they *would* see it. Faith allows us to have full assurance when we die that we will get to our final destination and enter the city that God prepared for us.

You may be the kind of person looking for some scientific proof of Heaven. You'll never find empirical evidence of Heaven in this world. If you're waiting until you see God to believe in Him, you'll see God but it will be too late then to believe. It's not that Christian faith is irrational; it is supra-rational. Theologian Elton Trueblood once wrote, **"Faith is not belief without proof. It is trust without reservation."** You must exchange your SIGHT for faith if you want to visit Heaven.

How do you spend the currency of faith?

The good news about the currency of Heaven is that you don't have to wait until you arrive in Heaven to spend it. We can spend it now while we're living here in this world! In fact, if you never use the currency of faith in this life, it will be too late to exchange Heaven's currency once you die. We must be willing to spend Heaven's currency in faith in order to see what God is doing in the world.

I've had many personal experiences with how this happens. I mentioned earlier when I visited Russia for the first time. On another trip there I encountered a situation where I had to ante up at the table of faith big time.

I led a group of about 40 volunteers from our church to conduct some mission work in the Crimea. We had a great trip. Our return flight that would connect through Moscow was late departing, so we were very late when we arrived at the domestic airport in Moscow. We still had to claim our luggage, load a bus, and then fight the congested Moscow traffic to arrive at the Sheremetyevo International Airport. We would have to go through security there, check our bags, and board. As the leader of the group, my stress level was clocking pretty high because it looked as if we would miss our flight to our next stop in Frankfurt, Germany, which would create an entirely new set of problems—namely, no hotel reservations or tickets for another flight.

When our bus arrived at the international airport in Moscow, our flight to Frankfurt was already boarding. From previous experience I knew that the check-in process for a group our size would take an hour. It seemed impossible. I whispered a quick but faith-loaded prayer,

40 Things You WON'T Find in Heaven

⑤ Tears

"Father, we need your help. I believe You want us to make this flight. But it will take a miracle."

When I said "amen," I saw a sight that made my heart sink. There was a long line of more than 500 people already lined up for security. And the line was creeping slowly. A part of me wanted to give up at that moment. All five senses told me that there was NO WAY that we would ever make the flight. But still, I had asked God to make a way.

We made our way to the end of the line and a young man came up to me. He was wearing light-blue coveralls, as if he worked at the airport. He asked in British-accented English, "Excuse me. May I help you?" His accent caught my attention because I wondered how a British man got a job working at the airport in Moscow.

I quickly explained our predicament and that we were about to miss the last flight out that evening. He smiled and

Travel Preview

JOHNNY C.

★ ★ ★ ★ ★

There will be no more sorrow, pain, or sickness. My wife had a tubular pregnancy that ruptured. She nearly died and was never able to conceive again. I believe that we will have a child when we get to Heaven.

calmly said, "Just follow me." Then he led our entire group pushing carts and pulling luggage right past the serpentine line of other travelers. He deposited us at the front of the line and spoke in perfect Russian to one of the Russian soldiers at the security checkpoint. The Russian soldier frowned but motioned us to go through *without a security check*!

We then arrived at the Lufthansa ticket counter and our group started collecting their luggage to be tagged. All the while our friend in the blue coveralls was cheerfully carrying pieces of luggage and placing them on the scales for the Lufthansa agents to process.

As the last member of our group walked down the jetway to board the flight to Frankfurt, I finally sighed with great relief. I said, "Thank you, Lord!" Then I reached into my pocket to offer a large cash gift to our friend who had helped us. But he was nowhere to be seen. It was a fairly large check-in area and I had seen him less than two minutes earlier lugging the last suitcase to the ticket agent.

I asked one of the agents, "Excuse me, but where is the young man in the blue coveralls who works for you? I wanted to give him a gratuity for his help." She had a puzzled look on her face and replied, "We don't have anyone matching that description who works for us."

I was confused and asked, "Didn't you see the guy loading the suitcases onto your scales a few minutes ago?" Again she looked puzzled and replied, "No, I'm sorry. I don't know who you're talking about." Then she resumed typing on her keyboard.

That's when I realized that perhaps God had sent one of his special "airport angels" to assist a group of American Christians who were desperately trying to get home. That's just a small example of the power of faith. You can't go by SIGHT. You have to go by FAITH.

40 Things You WON'T Find in Heaven

(6) Liars

Only faith accepted here

Are you starting to get the picture? All Heavenly transactions in this life—large and small—must be conducted the same way. By faith. For instance, think of prayer as if you are making a purchase. If you want to purchase an item that costs $100, you must produce $100 to complete the transaction. Prayer works the same way. When you ask God for something He requires FAITH as the payment.

Because you can't see faith, it's like having a Heavenly line of credit. In Romans 4:9 we learn, *"Abraham believed God and it was credited to Him as righteousness."* What does "credited" mean? If faith is Heaven's currency, then doubt is like going into spiritual debt. Jesus said, *"Have faith in God. Truly I tell you, if anyone says to this mountain, 'Be lifted up and thrown into the sea,' and does not doubt in his heart, but believes that what he says will happen, it will be done for him. Therefore I tell you, everything you pray and ask for—believe that you have received it and it will be yours"* (Luke 11:22-24).

It is NOT prayer alone that motivates God to move. It is faith that God values. That's why it doesn't matter how "well" you can pray—it's not the words you say; it's the faith you express. The most childlike prayer full of faith may not impress other people who hear it, but that's the kind of prayer that grabs God's attention.

So when you draw near to God in prayer, don't make a request without having the currency to back it up. Faith is the only thing of value that God accepts because it initially came from Him. We RECEIVED this faith when we allowed His Word to come alive in our hearts. The Bible says, *"Faith comes by hearing and hearing by the Word of God"* (Romans 10:17). When you spend money, you have less money to spend. But the currency of Heaven is exactly the opposite. The more faith you spend, the more faith you possess! So start using Heaven's currency today!

Getting to Heaven

One of the greatest leaps of faith you'll ever take is the one that comes at the end of your life and you trust in full assurance that you'll arrive safely in Heaven with Jesus. Contrary to popular belief, there is only one way to Heaven. I can't tell you the BEST route to Heaven; this travel guide can only point to the ONE way to Heaven. That's not only what the Bible teaches, it's also what Jesus said. Still, people have questions about routing their way to Heaven, and we'll take a look at the concerns in the next chapter.

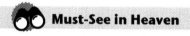 **Must-See in Heaven**

The Rainbow Around God's Throne

"The one seated there had the appearance of jasper and carnelian stone. A rainbow that had the appearance of an emerald surrounded the throne." — **REVELATION 4:3** (csb)

CHAPTER 3

WHICH ROUTE TO HEAVEN?

For years I was a private pilot. There was something about being able to roar down the runway and take off to soar in the sky that I loved. When I was a seminary student in Louisville, Kentucky, I started working on earning my pilot's license. I took a number of solo flights trying to build up enough hours to pass a "check-ride" with an FAA-approved examiner, the final step before receiving my license.

I took off from Bowman Field in Louisville one beautiful clear morning to make a 30-minute flight east to Lexington, Kentucky. I had a flight chart in my lap, but it was such a beautiful morning that I soon ignored the chart because I knew that the wide highway below me went to Lexington. So I just looked out the cockpit window and flew above the highway, content that I would soon arrive safely at my destination.

The air was smooth and the rolling green pastures below made for a wonderful flying experience. But as I was following the road, I soon saw a large river to my left. I glanced down at the chart and didn't see a river anywhere near my flight path. I felt better when I saw a city in the distance and assumed it was Lexington. But after a few confused moments of comparing the flight chart with the landscape below, I came to the sudden conclusion that I had followed the wrong highway out of Louisville. Instead I was heading for Cincinnati, Ohio!

I learned an important lesson that morning as a pilot. If I ignore the flight chart, no matter how confident I feel, I risk the danger of arriving at the wrong destination. The same is true when you want Heaven to be your final destination.

Is St. Peter really standing outside Heaven's gates?

There is no shortage of "jokes" about what it's like to arrive in Heaven. Usually people tell stories about St. Peter standing at the gates of Heaven, arbitrarily letting people inside.

40 Things You WON'T Find in Heaven

⑦ **False Doctrine**

Here's a good one. A man died and went to Heaven. St. Peter asked him, "Why should I let you into Heaven?" The guy said, "Well, I tried to help other people." "Can you give me an example?" St. Peter inquired. "Sure," the man said. "Once I was in a roadside diner and a group of Hell's Angels were bothering a little old lady. They had knives and guns and were scaring everyone in the place. So I stepped up to the leader, spun him around, and grabbed him by the collar of his leather jacket. I yelled, 'Hey! Why don't you leave that little lady alone? And while you're at it, you and your filthy friends should get on your bikes and leave right now!'"

St. Peter said, "Wow! That was pretty brave. When did that happen?"

Travel Preview

★★★★★

Having lost several very dear loved ones in recent years, I've been so struck with the realization that what appears to be a beautiful sunrise, sunset, or rainbow, from our perspective here must be absolutely breathtaking from their new perspective in Heaven!

BETH L.

The man said, "About two minutes ago!"

Most of the jokes about Heaven are NOT based on the truth of the Bible. They're funny but they can be misleading. For instance, there's nothing in the Bible that teaches St. Peter is going to meet people at the Pearly Gates and admit them into Heaven. Peter can't get you into Heaven— only Jesus can—and that's no joke.

How can I get to Heaven?

When you're planning a trip to a new destination, one of the first factors you consider is how to get there. Is there airline service? Can you take a train or a ship? Would it better to drive? If you're smart, you're not going to leave for your journey until you know the best way to get there.

There are countless religions in the world, and each one has a different idea of how to arrive safely into the afterlife. We live in a pluralistic society that preaches tolerance toward everyone—except those whom they consider to be intolerant. For example, it isn't politically correct to say that Jesus is the only way to Heaven in today's world. Do that and you might lose your job. You might lose friends. You might lose face in the eyes of the guys on the golf course or the ladies around the lunch table.

Therefore it's not surprising to know that the average American believes that there are many avenues to get to Heaven. They imagine it's like a 20-lane superhighway. Christians are driving in the Christian lane and others are driving in the Judaism lane. There's some in the Islam lane, and others in the Buddhist lane. But we're all going to arrive at the same destination—Heaven. Right?

> **Travel Tips** ✓
>
> ■ To arrive safely in Heaven, take the narrow path that leads to eternal life. (Matthew 7:13-14)

The only thing wrong with that idea is that it's wrong. Here's what Jesus said about that: "***Broad is the road that leads to destruction, and many enter through it. But small is the gate and narrow the road that leads to life, and only a few*** *find it"* (Matthew 7:13-14).

In John 14 Jesus talked about going back to His Father's house to prepare a PLACE for us. That's Heaven. Phillip was confused and asked Jesus, "Where are you going, and how can we know the way?"

40 Things You WON'T Find in Heaven

8 Political Debates

Jesus said, *"I am the way and the truth and the life. No one comes to the Father except through me"* (John 14:6). That's a pretty exclusive answer.

I once had a conversation with a man who told me that going to Heaven was like going to Chicago. He believed all religions were equal and even used the example of each religion representing a different airline company. He explained that a person could fly to Chicago on United Airlines, Delta Airlines, or American Airlines, but they would all arrive in Chicago.

He was right about getting to Chicago. However, I don't want Chicago to be my final destination! This is a travel guide to a much better place than that. I have my sights set on Heaven! In Psalm 90 the Bible speaks of the brevity of life. The Psalmist observed, *"Our lives last seventy years or, if we are strong eighty years... indeed they pass quickly and we fly away"* (Psalm 90:10). When it's your time to fly, there's only one transport to Heaven and He is Air Jesus!

Doesn't sincerity count for something?

Most people talk to me about spiritual things because they know I'm a pastor. They know that's my worldview, so they come in to my office with suppositions about what I believe because more often than not they are also Christians. It's a treat when I get to rub shoulders with people out in the world who have no idea of what I do for a living.

When I talk with folks who are not Christians, one of the most common reasons they give for not accepting Jesus as the only way to Heaven goes something like this: "It doesn't matter what you believe as long as you're SINCERE in your beliefs." Sincerity is not the same as veracity. You can be sincerely wrong. You can sincerely believe that you'll get to Oklahoma City from Dallas by driving west on Interstate 20, but you'll never get there using that route. If you're in Dallas, you must go north on Interstate 35 to get to OKC. Does that sound narrow minded? Does that seem intolerant of me to believe that? No, because it's a fact. It's the truth.

In the same way, Jesus was clear about the way to Heaven. He never claimed that He is ONE of the ways to Heaven. He never claimed to be a GOOD way to Heaven. He never insisted that He is even the BEST way to Heaven. He made the audacious claim that He is the ONLY way to Heaven.

 **Must-See in Heaven**

The River of Life

"Then he showed me the river of the water of life, clear as crystal, flowing from the throne of God and of the Lamb."
— REVELATION 22:1 (csb)

Religion vs. Relationship

You may be thinking, "Come on, Pastor David. Do you really think Jesus is that different than the other religious teachers?" You decide. Did any other religious teacher ever predict he or she would die and come back from the grave? Did any other religious teacher claim NOT ONLY to know the way to God...BUT ALSO to be equal with God? Did any other religious teacher claim to have been in existence before Abraham? And, for the clincher—did any other religious teacher actually die and come back from the dead?

Actually, Christianity is not a religion at all. It is not simply **following** the teachings of Jesus; it is rooted in having a personal relationship with Jesus. It means KNOWING your

Must-See in Heaven

The Great and High Mountain

"He then carried me away in the Spirit to a great, high mountain and showed me the holy city, Jerusalem, coming down out of heaven from God." — **REVELATION 21:10 (csb)**

Creator by knowing Jesus as your Lord and Savior, but also as your best friend who loves you more than you can imagine. We know Heaven is enjoying eternal life forever. But the Bible defines eternal life in an unexpected way. Instead of talking about living forever in a beautiful place, Jesus described eternal life in terms of a relationship when he prayed, *"This is eternal life: that they know you, the only true God, and the one you have sent—Jesus Christ"* (John 17:3).

You can be a Muslim by following the teachings of Mohammed. But it's impossible to KNOW him because he died on June 6, AD 632, and he's buried in Medina. You can be a Buddhist without KNOWING Buddha—in fact, he's also dead. He was cremated centuries ago. Some of his remains are in Sri Lanka. But I have taken many hundreds of my friends to an empty tomb in Jerusalem. They have stooped to walk into a tomb carved out of a limestone wall. Without fail, each one walks out of an empty tomb with full hearts shouting, "He is risen! He is risen indeed!" This is the God you can KNOW on a personal level through a relationship with His Son, Jesus.

 **Travel Preview**

★★★★★

The thought of standing face to face with Jesus, my Savior, who suffered and died for ME...I can't grasp that. But I am looking forward to it. I think that for the first time in my life, I'll be speechless!

SUZANNE F.

Is Heaven free?

Before planning a trip, it's important to determine the cost and make a budget. There are many factors to consider that will drive up the cost or save money. Will you drive or fly to your destination? Will you stay in a five-star hotel or camp out in a tent? A wise traveler will save up before traveling to make sure it's affordable. So what's the cost of traveling to Heaven? Will you have enough to cover it?

CHAPTER 4

THE COST OF TRAVEL

When my two daughters were young, we tried to plan some memorable vacations as a family. Because I was on a pastor's salary, we didn't have a lot of extra money. One year we decided on a Caribbean cruise. We started saving money every month and put it in a "cruise fund."

After saving carefully for about a year, we were ready to go. It was a trip of a lifetime for us and worth every penny. We boarded the Royal Caribbean *Sovereign of the Seas*, one of the largest cruise ships at the time. I had carefully budgeted the cost of the cruise and transportation to Miami to catch the ship. However, I had neglected one important detail.

An inexperienced cruiser, I failed to plan for all the onboard expenses! To my dismay, I quickly realized we had to pay extra for any excursions, all of our soft drinks, and many other items. We also had to leave generous tips for our cabin steward, server, and cruise director. I had way miscalculated the actual cost, so we spent months after the cruise saving more money to pay for these extras!

One ticket to Heaven, please

Some people believe that they have to pay their own way for the trip to Heaven through religious performance. So they spend their entire lives trying to "save up" for the trip.

For example, the second-largest religion in the world is

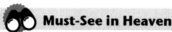 **Must-See in Heaven**

Elijah

Ask him about the time he rode a chariot into Heaven.

Islam. Followers of Islam hope to earn a place in Heaven based upon their goodness. They believe Allah may reward them with "Paradise" IF they faithfully follow the five pillars of Islam and perform more good deeds than bad. The Koran teaches that Allah has a set of Heavenly scales and if your good deeds outweigh the bad, you will be rewarded with Paradise.

For some people the idea of earning their way into Heaven takes an evil turn. In 2005 Barbara Walters interviewed different people around the world asking about their belief in Heaven or the afterlife. She interviewed a 17-year-old Palestinian terrorist who was a prisoner in a maximum-security prison in Israel. He had attempted to detonate a bomb strapped to his body on a busy street, but the bomb was a dud. Walters summarized his belief this way:

"He believes his reward will be to enter Paradise, where he will enjoy sex on silken couches with young virgins, amid rivers of milk and honey. Muslims believe that Paradise is a place of lavishly comfortable homes with beautiful gardens and servants to serve them. Food and wine will be plentiful, and both men and women will enjoy hedonistic pleasures.

 **Travel Preview**

MELODY S.

★★★★★

I know that the same God who made earth also made Heaven. Therefore I think of the awe-inspiring beauty of majestic mountains and a tropical paradise and I know that Heaven has to be so much more amazing!

As strange as it may seem, what drove this young man to attempt to commit his heinous act was his idea of Heaven and his longing to go there."

That's an extreme example of the everyday attitude many people have about EARNING access to Heaven. For example, some people think that they will win a trip to Heaven based upon how many times they attend church or take communion. Or they believe their eligibility for travel to Heaven is contingent on confessing every sin they've ever committed.

You can't pay your way to Heaven

I answered the phone one day and the cheery voice on the other line said that I had won a free trip to the Bahamas! It was my lucky day! Instead of hanging up on what I knew immediately was a scam, I decided to listen to the offer. Pastors are always looking for illustrations one way or another. The more I listened, the clearer the truth became.

First, in order to claim my prize, I had to give them some of my time to tour a resort and hear a sales pitch

Travel Tips

■ Don't rush to try to see everything. You have eternity to experience it. Take your time.

to buy a timeshare there. I also discovered that I had to pay for my own airfare. After all that, then I would indeed get three days and three nights of "free accommodation." So it wasn't a free trip at all, was it?

We each need a small dose of skepticism when it comes to things like that because there are plenty of scams out there for gullible people. But I'm afraid our skeptical modern culture has made it more difficult for people today to believe that someone could offer you something for free without having an ulterior motive. We live in an age of high-tech scammers, double-dealing, con games, and hustlers, and the last thing we want to do is fall for a shady deal.

Nevertheless, a free trip to Heaven is a rock-solid reality.

We can't pay our way to Heaven because the price has already been paid. It's free to us, but only because Jesus paid it all. And the price He paid came at a stunning cost. The Bible says, *"For you know that it was not with perishable things such as silver or gold that you were redeemed from your empty way of life handed down to you from your forefathers, but with the precious blood of Christ, a lamb without blemish or defect"* (1 Peter 1:18-19).

40 Things You WON'T Find in Heaven

(9) Depression

What's the catch?

There are several people in the church where I serve who perform a special ministry. Each year they donate funds for me to choose a pastor and his wife to take with me on a trip to Israel with a few dozen other travelers. A few years ago I was in Florida at a conference and met a young pastor and his wife at a banquet the first night. We ended up seated next to each other and in our conversation they casually mentioned that they'd really love to go Israel sometime.

I began to pray about it, and after the conference was over I called the young man and asked if they wanted to go to Israel with me on our annual church trip that year. His first question was, "How much will it cost?" I told him it was completely free.

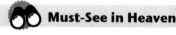

Must-See in Heaven

God's Temple in Heaven

"Then the temple of God in heaven was opened, and the ark of his covenant appeared in his temple. There were flashes of lightning, rumblings and peals of thunder, an earthquake, and severe hail."
— REVELATION 11:19 (csв)

But he had a hard time accepting the offer because it seemed too good to be true. We didn't really know each other that well and he wondered, "What's the catch?" I had to keep telling him there was no catch.

He even offered to pay part of the cost. I just laughed. This guy was not getting it! I finally convinced him that the trip was really free. All he had to do was say, "Yes."

Many hard-working Americans stumble over the fact that salvation is free. They want to work for it and somehow earn it, just as they do with a paycheck at their jobs. But Jesus has paid the full price. All you have to do is to say, "Yes" in faith to Jesus.

Ready to go?

What will Heaven be like? The Bible gives specific information on some things about the Heaven experience, and it leaves a lot to the imagination too. In this next section we'll talk about what happens to those of us who finally make that trip to Heaven and how life as we've always known it radically changes forever.

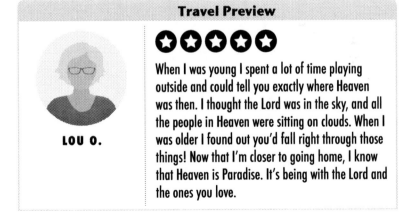

Travel Preview

⭐⭐⭐⭐⭐

When I was young I spent a lot of time playing outside and could tell you exactly where Heaven was then. I thought the Lord was in the sky, and all the people in Heaven were sitting on clouds. When I was older I found out you'd fall right through those things! Now that I'm closer to going home, I know that Heaven is Paradise. It's being with the Lord and the ones you love.

LOU O.

PART 2

MAKING THE TRIP TO HEAVEN

CHAPTER 5

AN OUT-OF-BODY EXPERIENCE

What do you think happens right after you die? There are many theories about what happens, but they usually fall into one of four categories. As we walk through each one, think of the friends, coworkers, college buddies, and/or family members you know who have said something like one or more of these ideas. Maybe there was a time when you yourself have even considered these perspectives.

First, there is a theory called materialism—it's another word for atheism. It basically teaches that when the body dies, that is the end of existence. There is nothing beyond. British author C. S. Lewis once commented on a tombstone in England that says, "Here lies an atheist. All dressed up with no place to go."

The second theory is reincarnation. Some of the Eastern religions teach that the soul survives after death, but it is reincarnated into another body. If the soul is enlightened it is reincarnated into a higher life form like a person. If not, it regresses into a lower animal form. Mark Twain once joked, "I don't believe in reincarnation—and I didn't believe in it in my former life, either."

The third theory about what happens after death is something called the Platonic theory of immortality. You may not have heard of it by that name, but you'll recognize the core beliefs. Plato suggested that the body is totally separate

Travel Preview

DANNA S.

⭐⭐⭐⭐⭐

Heaven will be a place like it was in the Garden of Eden. A place with beautiful trees and fruit on them of every kind. There will be flowers and birds singing. The lion and lamb will be sitting next to each other. Most of all, our Lord and Savior will be there along with all our loved ones with arms wide open to welcome us.

from the soul. In this dichotomy the body is bad and the soul is good. Death, therefore, is a welcome liberation of the soul from the confines of the inferior body. After death, the soul lives on without bodily form for eternity. Ghosts. Spirits. These kinds of movies and ghost-hunting documentaries are a mainstay today. Many Christians unknowingly embrace this Platonic belief. They think that they will become angels after they die. Or they will be floating around clouds in some ethereal experience forever.

Tell the truth

The fourth option for what happens to us after we die is what I'll call resurrection. The biblical teaching about resurrection is that at death, the soul and spirit leave the body. The body is buried and returns to the dust from which we're all formed. But at a future date, the Bible says, the body will be raised, radically changed, and reunited with the soul and spirit. Our existence in Heaven will be not just a physical experience—it will be a supra-physical experience.

Why soul AND spirit? What's the difference between the two? You and I are created in the image of God. That doesn't mean we look like God. But just as God is a tri-unity (meaning three expressions of the one God—Father, Son, and Spirit) we are a tri-unity as well. We are comprised of a body, soul, and spirit.

Before you come to know Christ, your spirit is dead. When

you become a Christian, your spirit becomes alive through the Holy Spirit who now dwells inside you. Your soul is your personality—mind, emotions, and will.

Trying to understand the differences between our body, soul, and spirit is often confusing. If you have trouble distinguishing between soul and spirit, that's normal. According to Hebrews 4:12, only the Word of God can separate the soul and spirit. C. S. Lewis once wrote, "You don't 'have' a soul. You *are* a soul. You *have* a body." That's true; the real essence of who we are is in our spirit, even though we tend to spend a lot of time, money, and attention on our bodies. But Jesus noted that the real value of a person is inside when He said, *"What shall it profit a man if he gains the whole world and loses his soul?"* (Mark 8:36)

40 Things You WON'T Find in Heaven

(10) **Worry**

Why do we have to die?

I heard the story of a pastor who was trying to impress upon his people the inevitably of death. He said one Sunday, "One day, every member of this church is going to die!" There was a young boy on the front row who laughed just as he said that statement. The pastor, thinking he misunderstood him, repeated it. "I said, 'One day, every member of this church is going to die!'" Again the boy laughed out loud. The irritated pastor asked, "Son, what's so funny about that?" The boy said, "I'm not a member of this church!"

One of the best passages dealing with what happens when we die is 2 Corinthians 5:1-9: *"For we know that if the earthly tent we live in is destroyed, we have a building from God, an eternal house in heaven, not built by human hands. Meanwhile we groan, longing to be clothed instead with our heavenly dwelling, because when we are clothed, we will not be found naked. For while we are in this tent, we groan and are burdened, because we do not wish to be unclothed but to be clothed instead with our heavenly*

40 Things You WON'T Find in Heaven

⑪ Fear

dwelling, so that what is mortal may be swallowed up by life. Now the one who has fashioned us for this very purpose is God, who has given us the Spirit as a deposit, guaranteeing what is to come.

"Therefore we are always confident and know that as long as we are at home in the body we are away from the Lord. For we live by faith, not by sight. We are confident, I say, and would prefer to be away from the body and at home with the Lord. So we make it our goal to please him, whether we are at home in the body or away from it."

We've determined that the outward person is your body, and the inward person is your soul and spirit. The real you (invisible to everyone but God) lives within a body just as a camper lives temporarily in a tent. Paul wrote about this tent being destroyed—that's a reference to death. It may be destroyed slowly by old age or by some disease. Or it could be destroyed suddenly as in someone having an automobile accident or a soldier being shot. We all die in different ways, but we all have one thing in common. This tent isn't permanent, and one day we'll move out of it.

What happens to the real me?

To put it another way, you have a visible, outward presence that is getting older every day as well as an invisible, inward presence that is ageless. When you look at me, you can only see the "outer me," but there is also an "inner me." That inner

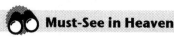

Must-See in Heaven

Beautiful White Horses

"The armies that were in heaven followed him on white horses, wearing pure white linen." – **REVELATION 19:14** (csb)

person is often called the ego, the personality, or the soul of a person. President Woodrow Wilson's favorite limerick was:

I know how ugly I are;
I know my face ain't no star.
But I don't mind it;
Cause I'm behind it.
It's the others who get the jar.

I don't have much control over the aging of the outer me. If you ask me, the man in the mirror looks a lot more like my father than the way I feel on the inside! I have a friend who is an oncologist who tells her patients, "If you want to live forever, you're in the wrong clinic." The human body is not designed to live forever. The Bible says, *"Therefore we do not lose heart. Though outwardly we are wasting away, yet inwardly we are being renewed day by day"* (2 Corinthians 4:16). As we grow older many of us can relate to this truth. We have a variety of aches and pains that come with age, but on the inside we still feel as we did when we were teenagers or young adults.

It reminds me of the Concorde aircraft. When this supersonic aircraft first flew transatlantic back in 1969 everyone thought it would revolutionize air travel. However, the beautiful Concorde took its last flight in 2003, and the aircraft has since been retired. Why? For the same reason our bodies wear out. It wasn't designed to last forever.

The Concorde could fly from London to New York in about three

Travel Tips

■ No smartphones or chargers needed. We'll all be together for eternity.

and a half hours instead of the six-hour trip today. It flew at a speed of 1,350 mph, twice the speed of sound, but the exterior of the plane was subjected to immense heat and pressure during flight. The exterior heated to an astonishing 216 degrees and the fuselage actually expanded in length by 10 inches compared to when it was on the ground! This

Travel Preview

DEBBIE N.

⭐⭐⭐⭐⭐

Heaven will be more beautiful than anything we have ever experienced or seen...we will all be healthy and happy forever and ever. We will know we are finally home.

tremendous pressure and heat led to structural fatigue and problems with the maintenance of the aircraft.

But no one traveling on the Concorde was ever aware of the wear-and-tear during flight. The interior space was maintained at a cool 69 degrees, and the passengers enjoyed the ride in comfort and luxury. Since they were traveling faster than sound, the cabin was extremely quiet. Outwardly the plane was under enormous stress, but inwardly it was fine. That's a picture of us living in our bodies. Outwardly we are under great pressure and strain living in a fallen world where sickness, sin, and disease assail us from all sides, and there will some day be a "material failure" one way or another. Barring the return of Jesus, we'll die one day. Meanwhile we are at peace inwardly—and, the Bible says, even getting better and better.

Here's the great truth. While your tent is getting more and more feeble, it's possible for your spirit to renew itself each day. I've lived for more than six decades in my tent, and every day there seems to be a few more aches and pains, but I'm more excited about living for Jesus than ever before.

Are we angels after we die?

I love the movie *It's a Wonderful Life* starring Jimmy Stewart. Frank Capra opens this classic flick with several people praying for George Bailey. George is in trouble and considering ending it all because some money is missing from the Savings and Loan where he works. Then the scene shifts to outer space where God is talking to an angel named Joseph.

God and Joseph summon an angel second-class named Clarence to go to earth and help out ol' George. Clarence is a man who died in the 1800s but he hasn't yet "earned his

40 Things You WON'T Find in Heaven

⑫ Kleenex

wings." Although he's not the brightest bulb in the socket, Clarence eventually succeeds in getting George to consider that his life is worth living. At the end of movie as George Bailey is standing by the Christmas tree, a bell on the tree rings. His little daughter Zuzu says the oft-quoted line, "Teacher says, 'Every time a bell rings, an angel gets its wings.'" And Jimmy Stewart smiles and says, "That's right. Attaboy, Clarence!"

That makes for a great movie, and believe me, I cry nearly every time I see Jimmy Stewart in this film (this and his classic *Shenandoah*, but that's another story). But the script distorts what the Bible says happens to a person when they die. We get a lot of our misconceptions about the afterlife from Hollywood and not nearly enough of what we believe about Heaven from the Bible.

The most popular misconception is that when a person dies, he or she becomes an angel like Clarence. Contrary to what so many people believe—even and especially well-meaning Christians—that just isn't true. One reason we know we don't become angels when we die is because of a story Jesus told in Luke 16 about a beggar named Lazarus. In this parable Jesus pulled back the veil from the afterlife and showed us a couple of truths about Heaven. When Lazarus died, Jesus said, the

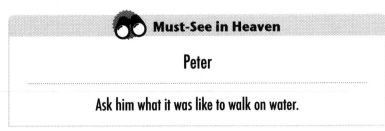

Must-See in Heaven

Peter

Ask him what it was like to walk on water.

angels carried him to Paradise. He had angels *accompany* him; he wasn't an angel himself!

Another reason we know that we don't become angels after death is because Jesus clearly addressed this topic. In Luke 20:35-36 Jesus answered a question about who would be married in Heaven. He used it as a teachable moment to explain what life would be like there. He said, *"But those who are considered worthy of taking part in the age to come and in the resurrection from the dead will neither marry nor be given in marriage, and they can no longer die; for they are like the angels. They are God's children, since they are children of the resurrection."* When Christians die, we don't become angels; we become something much greater. We are God's children.

> **Travel Tips**
>
> ■ No flashlights needed because the glory of God illuminates all of Heaven. (Revelation 21:23)

Many grieving parents mistakenly think that an infant who dies becomes a little angel. If you are a parent who has experienced this heartbreaking tragedy, I hope you'll be comforted to know that God has something even more extraordinary in store for your baby. Your child's Heavenly existence is much, much more wonderful than becoming an angel. He or she is now God's special child and very dear to His heart.

A few years ago a reader of *Decision Magazine* wrote a similar question to Billy Graham about this topic: *Dear Dr. Graham: My sister lost her small son a little over a year ago, and on the anniversary of his death, she put a poem in the paper to remember him. It said something about him being an angel now. Is that what happens to us when we die and go to Heaven, that we become angels? —Mrs. L.C.*

Billy Graham wrote back: *Dear Mrs. L.C.: I know your sister was sincere, and I respect her sorrow and her desire to remember and honor her son—but no, we don't become angels when we die and go to Heaven. The truth is, when*

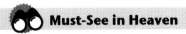 **Must-See in Heaven**

Moses

Ask him about walking through the middle of the Red Sea.

we die and go to Heaven, we become even greater than the angels! The angels are spiritual beings who were created by God to be His servants, and God has given them great authority and power to do His will. And at the present time, the angels are greater than we are, because God made us *"a little lower than the Heavenly beings"* (Psalm 8:5). But the Bible also says that in Heaven we will be higher than the angels—and the reason is because we will be like Christ. The Bible says, *"Do you not know that we will judge angels?"* (1 Corinthians 6:3) All of that, I know, may seem like theological hairsplitting to you. But don't lose sight of the central truth: When we know Christ, we know that this life is not all, but ahead of us is the joy of Heaven. May your sister take comfort in this truth and in the fact that her little son now is beyond all the pain and suffering of this world.

What's it going to be like?

So, if we're not reincarnated and we don't become angels, what will we look like in Heaven? What will our bodies in Heaven be like? Will we even have bodies? Let's take a look at all of this in the next chapter.

CHAPTER 6

EQUIPMENT FIT FOR HEAVEN

One of the most important steps to planning a trip is having and following a packing list. Based upon your destination you must decide, "What do I need to take?" When I travel alone or with a small group of guys, I never check a suitcase. Seriously, never. I can spend two weeks in Africa or Asia using only carry-on luggage and still have a fresh shirt every day. In order to do that I have to plan and pack carefully, and by now I am truly an expert packer!

When it comes to packing for Heaven, the key word is *relax*—there's nothing to carry with you. You really can't take anything with you anyway, though some have tried!

You've heard the story about the man who convinced the Lord to let him take just one suitcase with him to Heaven. So the guy converts all his assets into gold bullion, which he packs in a suitcase with instructions for it to be buried with him. When he dies he arrives at the Pearly Gates (you know that's not in the Bible, right?) and encounters a couple of angels. The angels say to the man, "We've got to check your suitcase before you enter Heaven."

So one of the angels opens the suitcase and finds the gold. The other angel leans over and asks, "What's in there?"

The first angel scratches his head in bewilderment and says, "Oh, it's just a pile of pavement!"

Streets of gold—now *that's* in the Bible!

You can't take anything with you, because everything you need will be provided for you in Heaven. A body. A home. Things to do. Just like you were given an earth suit (a physical body) to enjoy your time on earth, all the equipment you'll need to

40 Things You WON'T Find in Heaven

⑬ Hospitals

enjoy your time in Heaven starts with "trading up" for an eternal body.

Evidence that we'll have bodies in Heaven

Remember that Jesus told a story in Luke 16 about a beggar who died? In the story there was also a rich man whose name isn't given. In life the rich man mistreated Lazarus whenever he saw him. When Lazarus died the Bible says the angels carried him to Abraham's side. That's another description of Paradise. For any good Jew, joining Abraham would be a Heavenly experience. The rich man, however, died and woke up in Hades. I'll explain more in a moment, but the short story on Hades is that it is the underworld, which is like a temporary holding cell before hell. The rich man was suffering there, and to make matters worse, he could look into Paradise and see Lazarus and Abraham.

The rich man cried out, "Father Abraham. Have Lazarus dip his finger in water and come and touch my tongue for I am tormented in this flame." Interestingly, the rich man was still giving orders to Lazarus, even in death.

What I want you to notice in this parable about the immediate afterlife is that the rich man had a sense of a body—he could see and recognize Lazarus. He understood that Lazarus had a finger and he had a tongue. He also had the physical sense of suffering. Based upon these details I believe that our interim Heavenly bodies will have things we're used to on earth like fingers and tongues. We'll be able to experience physical sensations.

As I said, the rich man wasn't yet in hell; he was in a place called Hades—which is hellish in nature. Revelation 20 says that at the end of time, death and Hades will deliver up the dead in them. Anyone whose name is not found written in the Book of Life will be cast into the lake of fire, which is something the Bible calls "the second death." Think of Hades like the county jail before a prisoner is sentenced to the federal penitentiary in hell with no parole.

By the same token, Lazarus wasn't yet in the final Heaven. The Bible says he was in Paradise, the current Heaven. Paradise is like the entrance resort to our final Heaven—it is Heavenly in nature. Some call Paradise pre-Heaven, or the intermediate state, but I prefer to call it Paradise.

So what about Christians who have died?

This is a point of confusion for many Christians. Let me try to explain by using my dad as an example. My dad died on May 29, 1981, at 7:15 P.M. He was 58 years old. He died of cancer while he was a patient at the Mobile Infirmary in Mobile, Alabama. At 7:15 and one nanosecond, his soul and spirit departed from his cancer-riddled body—a tent that was very broken and tattered. He woke up in Paradise in the presence of Jesus, Abraham, and many others with a sense of a body that was whole and well. Like Lazarus and the rich man he had a sense of having a finger and a tongue like he had on earth, and he was aware of his surroundings.

Meanwhile, we took my father's corpse and buried it in Panama City, Florida, per his wishes. That's where his body has remained since 1981. That tent is probably in worse

Travel Preview

⭐⭐⭐⭐⭐

I believe Heaven to be a time of pure joy, praising God in the company of family, friends, and all the saints. We will not remember sorrow or pain. We will never be hungry, or tired, or sick. There will be no questions in our minds. We will have been made whole.

JEFF P.

shape than when we buried it, but that's okay. When I think of the bodies of dead believers, my mind goes back to some of the brave believers in the first century who were burned at the stake or eaten alive by animals in the Roman Colosseum. There wasn't much left of their bodies to start with, never mind the centuries of decay. Other Christians were lost at sea, beheaded, or buried so long ago that their bodies have turned to dust by now. But don't focus on the condition of those tents; think about the inner nature of those faithful ones. Every bit of who they are is safe with Jesus in Paradise now, with a wonderful sense of having a healthy body for the interim that works great and is perfectly suited for them.

My dad is joyful and content in Paradise, but he knows that the body he has now in Paradise isn't his permanent Heavenly body. How does he know that? He and every believer in Heaven knows that an essential event described in Scripture has not yet happened. One day Jesus is going to return in the clouds to rapture the Church. When Jesus comes, the Bible says He will bring the saints (including my dad!) with Him. That's when the Bible tells us that they'll get their final, eternal resurrection bodies as the dead in Christ all over the world are raised the meet the Lord.

The Bible says, *"For we believe that Jesus died and rose again, and so we believe that God will bring with Jesus those who have fallen asleep in him...For the Lord himself will come down from heaven, with a loud command,*

> **Travel Tips**
>
> ■ Pack light—you can't take it with you. In fact, you don't even need to pack!

with the voice of the archangel and with the trumpet call of God, and the dead in Christ will rise first. After that, we who are still alive and are left will be caught up [that's the Latin word *raptio*, or *rapture*] *together with them in the clouds to meet the Lord in the air. And so we will be with the Lord forever"* (1 Thessalonians 4:14-17).

I've written another book called *Revelation: God's Final Word* that explains in greater detail the Rapture and the events leading up to, during, and after it. But for the sake of helping you plan your trip to Heaven, let me cover the basics in rapid fashion.

At the Rapture, the resurrected saints and those who are alive at the return of Jesus will join Him in this Paradise. We'll all be together there, according to my understanding of Daniel and Revelation, for seven years. Then when Jesus returns at the final battle of Jerusalem, we'll all come back to earth with Him. It will be a short battle, one where the Bible says Jesus will win with the sword that comes out from His mouth. In other words, He only has to speak one word such as "Victory!" and the battle will be finished.

Then Jesus will rule and reign on earth for 1,000 years, and we'll be there with Him for that time. At the end of the thousand years, God will create a new Heaven and a new earth. It will be the greatest total makeover ever. As beautiful and wondrous as some places on earth are, you ain't seen nothing yet. That's when the New Jerusalem will descend from Heaven to earth—and that's when we will begin to experience the permanent Heaven forever and ever.

Is my loved one okay?

Whew. That was a fast overview of the most significant events that await us in the future. But this raises a good question. You may be thinking, "Isn't it tough on your dad and others in Heaven as they are waiting for their resurrection bodies?"

Not at all.

First, I don't even think they have a sense of waiting for a long time. When a believer dies and enters Paradise, time and space are meaningless. With God, the Bible says, a day is like a thousand years and a thousand years is like a day. There are no clocks in Paradise.

Second, as I've said earlier in this chapter, I believe the Bible gives evidence that they already have a sense of a physical body for the interim—one that has the full expression of at least our five senses.

Third, we don't have to worry that God will leave our loved

ones in a lurch or with anything less than exactly what they need to be happy while they wait for us to join them one day. Remember, we're returning to the One who lovingly made us in the first place—He knows how to care for us for eternity far better than we do.

What if I'm alive when Jesus returns?

So what happens to the generation of Christians who are alive when Jesus returns? The Bible indicates that they won't experience death. They will go straight to Paradise without going through a cemetery. I believe that I will be among that generation because I've held a lifelong conviction that Jesus is returning in my lifetime. I may be wrong about that, but in the meantime I'm not looking for the undertaker. I'm looking for the uppertaker!

 Must-See in Heaven

The Four Living Creatures

"Something like a sea of glass, similar to crystal, was also before the throne. Four living creatures covered with eyes in front and in back were around the throne on each side. The first living creature was like a lion; the second living creature was like an ox; the third living creature had a face like a man; and the fourth living creature was like a flying eagle. Each of the four living creatures had six wings; they were covered with eyes around and inside. Day and night they never stop, saying: Holy, holy, holy, Lord God, the Almighty, who was, who is, and who is to come. Whenever the living creatures give glory, honor, and thanks to the one seated on the throne, the one who lives forever and ever, the twenty-four elders fall down before the one seated on the throne and worship the one who lives forever and ever. They cast their crowns before the throne, and say: Our Lord and God, you are worthy to receive glory and honor and power, because You have created all things, and by your will they exist and were created."

— REVELATION 4:6-11 (csb)

In the Old Testament, Enoch gives us a beautiful picture of Jesus returning to rapture the church. Enoch is one of only two men in the Bible who didn't experience physical death. The other was Elijah, who was carried alive into Heaven in a chariot

40 Things You WON'T Find in Heaven

(14) Medicine

of fire. The writer of Hebrews described Enoch's non-death experience in these words: *"By faith Enoch was taken from this life, so that he did not experience death: 'He could not be found, because God had taken him away.' For before he was taken, he was commended as one who pleased God"* (Hebrews 11:5).

Enoch was a man who walked with God and one day he simply disappeared. I picture God and Enoch walking together in the cool of evening at sunset, talking to each other. When it was time for Enoch to go back home, I imagine God saying, "Hey Enoch—we're closer to My House now than yours. Why don't you just come home with Me tonight?"

Suddenly Enoch was no longer present on earth.

The same thing will happen to millions of Christians when Jesus comes to rapture the church. We will simply disappear. The King James Version says that Enoch was "translated." The Greek word in Hebrews 11:5 is the basis of our English word *metathesis*, which means "to exchange." A metathesis is when you exchange one letter for another in a word. The best example of a metathesis is the celebrity Oprah Winfrey. Her real name is Orpah from the book of Ruth, but everyone in her family exchanged the letters and called her Oprah. That's a metathesis—a change. When a person incorrectly says, "perscription" rather than "prescription," that's a metathesis. It's a change from one thing to another. Enoch "exchanged" one location for another. He exchanged earth for Heaven—that's a great exchange!

It is also a word that also means to transpose music. Sometimes when a person wants to sing a song in a higher key, a musician will transpose the music into a higher key.

That's what happened to Enoch, and that's what will happen to us who are alive at the coming of the Lord. We'll be transposed into a higher key—a MUCH higher key!

40 Things You WON'T Find in Heaven

(15) Tooth Cavities

I hope that the passage in 1 Corinthians 15 begins to make more sense now. The Bible says (parentheses mine), *"Listen, I tell you a mystery: We will not all sleep (the dead), but we (the living) will all be changed. In a flash, in the twinkling of an eye, at the last trumpet (the signal for the Rapture). For the trumpet will sound, the dead will be raised imperishable, and we (the living) will be changed. For the perishable (the dead) must clothe itself with the imperishable, and the mortal (the living) with immortality."*

After Jesus returns, we will have our permanent resurrection bodies. What will that be like for eternity? The following are some truths based on what the Bible teaches.

Mentally, you'll have a peaceful mind

When you have your permanent resurrection body, you'll have the mind of Christ. Have you ever struggled to remember something? Or searched for the right word and stuttered trying to find it? Have you ever made a mistake and beat yourself up by saying, "How can I be so dumb?" In Heaven we will be mentally perfect. Paul wrote, *"Now I know in part, then I shall know fully, even as I am known"* (1 Corinthians 13:12).

We all have questions now with no answers. Why is there cancer? Why do good people die young? Why are there tornados and earthquakes? We'll never have the answers in this life, but when we meet Jesus we won't even have to ask Him. We'll KNOW even as we are known. We will have absolute mental peace.

It seems that I've been a student all my life. When I first started studying algebra in the ninth grade, the teacher seemed to be speaking a foreign language. What in the world were "x" and "y?" And why should I care? For weeks I was totally confused. Then one day it clicked for me. I realized that "x" and "y" could be any number based upon the other numbers in the equation. They were just variables. Wow! From that time on, I tackled algebra and other math courses with confidence and enthusiasm. It became one of my favorite subjects. I even scored a perfect 36 in math on my ACT college entrance exam. (But I haven't used much algebra since!)

Have you ever been puzzled with a mental challenge that seemed unsolvable? Then somehow you had that "aha" moment when everything fell into place? In Heaven there will be no confusion and no misunderstandings. Having the mind of Christ, you will understand all knowledge and wisdom in an instant. It will be an overwhelming and satisfying "aha" moment that will last for eternity!

The Bible says that we look at life now as if "through a glass darkly." Things that bothered us so much on Earth will seem so trivial in Heaven. If your loved one was haunted by PTSD, addiction, dementia, Alzheimer's disease, depression, or even just bad memories from childhood—you can be sure that all that has been washed away. Things they dwelled on when they lived here never even cross their minds there. It's all forgiven, forgotten, and forever erased. We don't have lobotomies when we arrive in Heaven—it's just that mentally, we're perfect. We have perfect knowledge—and the wisdom to understand what we know.

Emotionally, you'll have a joyful heart

There are times in this life we are ecstatically happy, and other times when we sink into the depths of despair. As Frank Sinatra once sang, that's life. Our emotions can be a roller coaster that alternates between highs and lows. There are times when we are angry, and other times when we worry ourselves sick.

But in Heaven there will be none of those negative emotions. There will be constant and pure joy. You know that feeling when you are so full of joy that your face hurts from smiling and you think you might burst? That's what it will be like forever. The Bible says, *"In your presence is fullness of joy"* (Psalm 16:11).

In Heaven the party has already started. In Luke 15 Jesus told us that our Father is like a loving Shepherd who leaves 99 sheep inside the fence to go searching for the one lost lamb that He loves. Then He said that there is *"more rejoicing in Heaven over one sinner who repents than over ninety-nine righteous persons who do not need to repent"* (Luke 15:7). Of course Jesus made that statement with a twinkle in His eye because He knew that EVERYONE needs to repent. With so many thousands of people becoming Christians every day throughout the world in every nation, there is a lot of rejoicing going on in Heaven. And your loved one is smack dab in the middle of that party having the time of his or her life.

So take a moment and think about the most joyful moment of your earthly life. Maybe it was when you were married. It might have been when you had your first child. It might have been on the way home after spending the day with family and friends at a happy gathering. Hang on to that sense of joy and multiply it a zillion times and you'll come close to the kind of joy you will experience every moment of Heaven.

Travel Preview

★★★★★

Growing up, I would visit my grandmother for the summers. When I arrived, she had my room ready with everything I could want...the perfect pillow, my favorite colors, all just for me. In her kitchen were all my favorite foods. I knew total unconditional love. God not only loves me but He has also prepared a place for me. And that place is Heaven.

JUDY T.

Physically, you'll have a perfect body

40 Things You WON'T Find in Heaven

⑯ Divorce

Have no doubt—we will have a REAL physical experience for all eternity. Why is that? Because we were made to have bodies! It's like when you take something to the UPS store to be mailed. There are boxes, paper envelopes, padded envelopes, packing peanuts, tape, etc. available to protect your precious package. You don't just plop your item into the mail slot unprotected. If you care about what you're mailing you put it in a padded envelope or in a box with peanuts and tape it up tight.

In the same way, God chose the perfect covering for the "real you" to be in for your time on earth. He could have created Adam and Eve any way He wanted—but He chose to put us into earth suits—our bodies. He lovingly knit us together in our mothers' wombs with a system so delicate and complex that science has barely scratched the surface of discovering the mystery of how it all works. He cares for us throughout our lives, and for some of us, He has even miraculously healed our bodies so that they don't wear out prematurely. God loves the human body because He designed it, and Scripture assures us that even after death He's not through with it yet.

What will the resurrected body be like?

It's natural to be curious about what our resurrected bodies will be like. The Bible keeps a lot of the information under wraps, but it also contains enough clues to answer some of our questions about what life will be like then, mainly from the example of the resurrected Jesus.

The Bible says, *"We know that when Christ appears, we shall be like him, for we shall see him as he is"* (1 John 3:2). These bodies that hurt, wear out, and ache will be transformed into a body like Jesus had after His resurrection.

When Jesus appeared in the Upper Room on the first Easter, the disciples were frightened. They thought it was a ghost. I can just see Jesus looking amused at them and saying, *"'Why are you frightened? Look at my hands and my feet. It is I myself. Touch me and see; a ghost does not have flesh and bones as you see I have.' Then he said, 'Do you have anything to eat?' They gave him a piece of broiled fish, and he took it and ate it in their presence"* (Luke 24:39-43).

After He was resurrected from the dead, Jesus had a body that the disciples saw, touched, and held. He even ate food to prove to them that he was real. What this teaches me is that we won't be blobs of plasma or ghostlike specters. Instead our resurrection bodies will be like Christ's.

(1) Our resurrection bodies will be much like the nature of our current bodies. In 1 Corinthians 15 Paul talks about our bodies as a seed that is planted. God's not going to resurrect our physical bodies just to transform them into orbs that float on clouds. We will have flesh and bones like Jesus did after the resurrection.

People often ask me if we will recognize our loved ones in Heaven. I believe so. Jesus met the disciples at the Sea of Galilee after His resurrection. Peter recognized Him immediately and swam to Him. I imagine they embraced and Peter

40 Things You WON'T Find in Heaven

⑰ Insurance

felt the wonderful feeling of hugging someone he'd missed and loved very much.

(2) Our resurrection bodies will be enhanced. They will be a cut above our current bodies because they will be designed for life in Heaven. When you think of the limitations of our current bodies and the limitless possibilities of Heaven, you'll realize there is really no comparison between what we have now and what we'll enjoy one day. Jesus appeared with the two disciples at Emmaus, and then He disappeared. That same evening the disciples were hiding behind locked doors in Jerusalem and Jesus appeared in their midst without going through the door. Later that night He disappeared without using the door. Since the Bible says, "we will be like Jesus" then, I believe that we will have senses and abilities that will be greatly enhanced from anything we have experienced in this body on earth.

So not only will we maintain our five senses, they will be supercharged. For instance, we will gaze into the eyes of our loved ones and see things we've never seen before. We will know them better than we've ever known them. In this life, dogs can hear and smell much better than us. In Heaven, I believe our senses will be enhanced beyond our imagination.

I was at a conference recently and the speaker was talking about greeting our loved ones who are in Heaven. He said that he believes we'll be able to hug them and even smell the unique fragrance of our loved ones. I smiled when he said that because I thought of several widows in our church who would give anything to breathe in the comforting scent of their loved one just one more time. In Heaven we will hug them and be able to recognize their familiar smell for eternity.

(3) Our resurrection bodies will not be subjected to the weaknesses we now have. So how old will we be in Heaven? Some have suggested that we'll be 33 years old—the age of Jesus when He was crucified. But the Bible never teaches that. That's just speculation. I believe we will each be the PERFECT age. Infants and elderly won't have to struggle with the shortcomings of immaturity or senility. We'll all be the PERFECT age to experience no more pain, no more suffering, no more death.

The Bible never says how old we will be for eternity, but you will always be the perfect age for vitality and health. J. Oswald Sanders wrote in a book called *Heaven: Better by Far*, **"We will have bodies fit for the full life of God to indwell and express itself forever. We will be able to eat but will not need to. We will be able to move rapidly through space and matter. We will be ageless and not know pain, tears, sorrow, sickness, or death. We will have bodies of splendor."**

What will happen at your funeral?

In more than 40 years of serving as a pastor I have conducted many hundreds of funerals. The very toughest funerals I have ever conducted are for those who never indicated any interest in God or the church. Now, I realize that I'm not the final judge of who is saved and lost—that position has been filled for eternity. I never assume that a person didn't go to Heaven. That's God's domain. But I have observed the deep, bottomless kind of grief that is expressed at funerals where the deceased gave no evidence of walking with God. I have often been brought to tears myself as I observe family members wailing over the death of someone who never gave any visible evidence of faith.

There is a dramatic contrast between that kind of grief and the grief expressed at the funeral of a man or woman who obviously walked with God. In 1 Thessalonians 4:13, the apostle Paul identifies the difference. He wrote, *"Brothers and sisters, we do not want you to be uninformed about those who sleep in death, so that you do not grieve like the rest of mankind, who have no hope."* Funeral services are designed to give encouragement and comfort to a grieving family. When a Christian dies there is grief, but it is infused with HOPE. At the funeral of someone who gave no evidence of salvation there is HOPELESS grief.

For instance, just a few weeks before writing this chapter I participated in the funeral service of a 92-year-old man who had been a faithful servant of the Lord for most of his life. There were tears because his loved ones missed him terribly, but there was a lot more laughter and smiles as people told stories about the obvious faith of this gentleman. Everyone there had a sense that they would see him in Heaven one day.

So what is going to be the attitude of people attending your funeral? If you know Jesus and serve Him joyfully, then your funeral will be a celebration of life well lived!

Death is waiting

Death is not a popular subject. But in order to get to Heaven, unless Jesus returns, you have to die first. This is the subject of the next chapter. How should we face the actual experience of death? For a Christian, death does not need to be an ominous, scary prospect. It is something we can face with as much confidence as we have when we leave one room and walk into another.

 Must-See in Heaven

Seven Burning Lamps

"Flashes of lightning and rumblings and peals of thunder came from the throne. Seven fiery torches were burning before the throne, which are the seven spirits of God." — **REVELATION 4:5** (csb)

CHAPTER 7

NO CAMPING ALLOWED

I will admit that I don't really care for sleeping in a tent on the hard ground. The last time I camped out was when my daughters were young and we spent a summer vacation in Angel Fire, New Mexico. A local company offered an overnight horseback ride up in the mountains. My wife declined, so I took our girls by myself. We rode horses all day up the steep trails toward the mountain peaks. Before long my thighs were hurting and I was thinking maybe my wife had the better idea. But I tried to focus on the fact that at least the evening air was cooler as we went higher into the mountains.

We stopped before sunset to set up camp and erected our tent as the trail hands prepared supper over a fire. We had a wonderful meal and sat around telling stories. Just before we turned in for bed, one of the trail hands loaded all the leftovers and garbage into a strong metal box bolted to a large tree.

My younger daughter asked, "What's that for?"

"That's so the bears can't get into the food," he replied.

Both my daughters looked at me with eyes full of fear. I quickly replied to the guy, "But you probably don't see too many bears around here, do you?"

The trail hand wasn't getting my drift. He just frowned and said, "Well, some nights they wander up when they catch a scent of the food. But don't worry, the horses will usually start making noise if a bear is near."

With that we went inside our tent and both girls pulled their sleeping bags right next to mine. None of us slept much because the horses made noises all night, and we all sat up wondering if a bear was near! That

40 Things You WON'T Find in Heaven

(18) Car Wrecks

was my last camping experience, and I was glad to get back to the world of beds and indoor plumbing!

Why we don't have to fear death

We already talked about how our bodies wear out like an old tent. But there's something else about a tent that teaches us about death and dying. The main thing to understand from Paul's illustration (who was a tentmaker, by the way) is that a tent is a TEMPORARY dwelling. We're here on earth temporarily. But I'm glad to say that we won't have campouts in Heaven. We never have to pack up and leave. Heaven involves dwelling in a permanent body for eternity. The instant we die we fold up and leave this earthly tent to be in the presence of Jesus in Paradise forever.

The best and shortest description of the death of a Christian in the Bible is 2 Corinthians 5:8, which says, *"Away from the body and at home with the Lord."* You may be familiar with the King James translation, which reads, *"Absent from the body, present with the Lord."* The word for "death" in the Hebrew language literally means, "to breathe out." It's similar to our English word "expire." The Bible says in John 19:30 that when Jesus died on the cross He said, *"'It is finished.' With that Jesus bowed his head and gave up his spirit."* That's how quickly we are separated from our bodies and with the Lord—after the last breath we take on earth, the next breath we take is in Heaven.

When death is a good thing

Death for a Christian is departing from the best this life has to offer to be with Jesus, which is much, much, much better by far. When Paul wrote to Timothy near the end of his life he said, "The time of my departure is at hand." Paul chose this word *departure* to describe a soldier who breaks camp and folds up his tent to move on to another assignment. It is also a word used to describe a prisoner set free from his chains.

Dwight L. Moody was the Billy Graham of the 19th century. He led crusades in North America and England where thousands of people accepted Christ. Moody Bible Church and Moody Bible Institute in Chicago are named after him. Here's how he described death: "**Someday you will read in the papers, 'D. L. Moody of East Northfield is dead.' Don't you believe a word of it! At that moment, I shall be more alive than I am now; I shall have gone up higher, that is all, out of this old clay tenement into a house that is immortal—a body that death cannot touch, that sin cannot taint; a body fashioned like unto His glorious body. I was born of the flesh in 1837. I was born of the Spirit in 1856. That which is born of the flesh may die. That which is born of the Spirit will live forever.**"

Travel Preview

CINDY R.

Heaven will be more peaceful than a secluded beach on a gorgeous day with gently rolling ocean waves. It will be more brilliant than any dazzling picture that NASA has ever shared of the stars. The feast we shall enjoy will be such a treat that even the most notable culinary experts' best recipes cannot compare. Heaven will be full of mansions grander than the wealthiest human could ever have built...but it will feel like my inviting, cozy home when it's my turn to go there.

How should I face death?

A Christian shouldn't fear death. One of my favorite descriptions of the godly woman from Proverbs 31 is that *"She can laugh at the days to come"* (Proverbs 31:25). Though death is no laughing matter, Christians can inject a little humor into the somber atmosphere of death. An inscription on a tombstone is called an epitaph, and through the years I've enjoyed collecting humorous epitaphs. Call it a preacher's hobby. Here are some of my favorites:

On a tombstone in Ribbesford, England: **"Here lies Anna Wallace; The children of Israel wanted bread; And the Lord sent them manna; Old clerk Wallace wanted a wife; And the Devil sent him Anna."**

On a tombstone in Ruidoso, New Mexico: **"Here lies Johnny Yeast; Pardon me for not rising."**

On a tombstone in Richmond, Virginia: **"She always said her feet were killing her; But nobody believed her."**

On a tombstone in Portland, Maine: **"Here lies my wife; I bid her good-bye. She rests in peace; And now so do I."**

My all-time favorite is from a tombstone in Nantucket, Massachusetts, because it really describes what happens to a Christian at death: **"Under the sod; And under the trees; Lies the body; Of Jonathan Pease. But Pease isn't here; This is just the pod; Peas shelled out; And went to God."**

 **Must-See in Heaven**

A Pile of Crowns around the Throne

"...the twenty-four elders fall down before the one seated on the throne and worship the one who lives forever and ever. They cast their crowns before the throne and say, Our Lord and God, you are worthy to receive glory and honor and power, because you have created all things, and by your will they exist and were created."
— REVELATION 4:10-11 (csb)

I've read about a tombstone in Georgia that reads: "Remember young man, as you pass by; As you are now, so once was I. As I am now, you soon shall be. So prepare, young man, to follow me."

Travel Tips

■ Don't worry about setting your watch to Heaven time—time will be no more.

According to the story, someone added a postscript to the tombstone that said, "To follow you is not my intent. Until I know which way you went!"

Where will you be five seconds after you die?

I believe there are only three possible honest answers to this question.

(1) There is a CONFIDENT response: "I will be with Jesus in Heaven."

That's how Paul would have answered. I would use those same seven simple words. If you ask some fellow preachers they would give you a much lengthier reply, but they would still be saying that same answer.

Can you, at this moment, honestly and confidently answer with those seven words? If you can't, then your honest answer will be one of the remaining two replies.

(2) There is a CONFUSED response: "I don't know."

Now that's an honest answer because there are people who really DON'T know what will happen after they die. You may be one who, when asked that question, responds by saying, "I don't know—I hope so. I think so." What you mean is you're really not sure, but you're hoping and wishing that you'll make it to Heaven.

The people in this category fall into two groups. One group may be Christians who just don't have a sense of assurance of their salvation. I'll talk more about confirming your reservation in Heaven in a later chapter. But there is another group of people who sincerely don't know what the Bible teaches about eternal life. There are still many people in America who have never been told the Gospel.

It's the Christians' job to TELL them the truth of the Gospel.

Here's what I tell those who honestly don't know where they'll be after they die: "The Bible teaches that there are only two eternal destinations. You'll either die in Christ and go to Heaven for eternity, or you'll die in your sins and go to a

40 Things You WON'T Find in Heaven

⑲ **Jealousy**

place of eternal separation from God in a place called hell. But God loves YOU so much that He sent His one and only Son, Jesus, to die on the cross for your sins. If you'll believe in Him, you'll never perish, instead you'll have eternal life."

Once I've explained that to people who honestly didn't know before, they immediately disappear from this group. Because now they *know*! At that point they'll either seek to trust Jesus as their Lord and move up to answer #1, or they will reject the truth and move to the only other possible honest answer:

(3) There is a CALLOUSED response: "I don't care."

Some people's hearts have become so hardened to the Gospel they have allowed callouses to grow around their heart. They have no interest or desire to know God and to be in Heaven. They don't simply reject the truth; they do worse than that—they *ignore* it. Their response to the question is, "Big deal. I don't care." But that's not really an honest answer, because the time will come when they care very much. Five seconds after they die, it will be the ONLY thing that they care about.

I love the story about the little girl who walked home from school every day. Her route took her through the local cemetery. She loved to feel the breezes, hear the birds, and enjoy the silence in the cemetery. Sometimes she would just lie on her back in the grass and watch the shapes of the clouds change. Other times she would skip through the cemetery singing songs and whistling her favorite tunes. She often paused and read the names and dates of people on the tombstones and imagined their stories. One day one of her friends said, "Why do you walk through the cemetery every

Travel Preview

⭐⭐⭐⭐⭐

I will get a new relationship with Jesus! Oh, my. So longing for a hug and a gentle touch from Him. I will get to talk to Him, meet and relate to Him face to face, as well as meet the great characters of the Bible.

SARAH C.

day? Aren't you afraid?" The little girl answered, "No, I'm not afraid. It's just the best way home."

Going home

Almost everyone goes through life with a partial sense of dissatisfaction. We're looking for the "it" experience. And we're not even sure what the "it" is. People attempt all kinds of thrills and experiences and even blow through relationships to see if that's "it," only to find out that it's not "it." I believe the "it" we're all looking for is being with God in Heaven. C. S. Lewis wrote: **"If I find in myself desires which nothing in this world can satisfy, the only logical explanation is that I was made for another world."**

In the *Wizard of Oz* Dorothy clicked the heels of her ruby slippers together three times and said, "There's no place like home. There's no place like home." We've adopted that phrase into our American mentality. We go on trips and vacations, but we're always longing to get home...even if home isn't as nice as that resort and there are problems and challenges awaiting us when we return. There truly is no place like home. If you're a follower of Jesus Christ, I want to remind you that you aren't home—yet.

> Think of stepping on shore and finding it Heaven;
> Of taking hold of a hand and finding it God's;
> Of breathing new air and finding it celestial air;
> Of feeling invigorated and finding it immortality!
> Of passing from storm and stress to a perfect calm;

Of waking and finding it HOME!
—Author unknown

Heaven's daily activity schedule

So what do you imagine you'll be doing in Heaven...for eternity? Singing hymns...for eternity? Playing golf...for eternity? If you've ever traveled in a group, you are familiar with a daily activity guide that outlines what all you're going to do for the day. I hope you'll dog-ear this next section in the travel guide because it's all about what the Bible says we'll really be doing in Heaven. And I bet you may find some of it surprising.

 **Must-See in Heaven**

The Ark of the Covenant

"Then the temple of God in heaven was opened, and the ark of his covenant appeared in his temple. There were flashes of lightning, rumblings and peals of thunder, an earthquake, and severe hail."
— REVELATION 11:19 (csb)

PART 3

HEAVEN'S ACTIVITY GUIDE

CHAPTER 8

EXPLORING HEAVEN

You can rely on a travel guide to tell you the best places to stay and the best places to eat, and provide a list of don't-miss activities and attractions. Heaven isn't designed as a vacation. It's an eternal destination. So, what is there to do in Jesus' hometown?

Perhaps the biggest falsehood that people have about Heaven is that it will be boring.

I remember a *Far Side* cartoon by Gary Larson where there's a guy sitting alone on a cloud. He has wings, a white robe, and a halo. He is obviously bored, and he is thinking, "I wish I'd brought a magazine!"

Heaven is anything BUT boring!

In *The Adventures of Huckleberry Finn*, Huck expresses a similar observation about Heaven that I'm afraid many people relate to: "**She [Miss Watson] told me all about the good place. She said all a body would have to do there was to go around all day long with a harp and sing, forever and ever. I asked her if she reckoned Tom Sawyer would go there, and she said, not by a considerable sight. I was glad about that, because I wanted him and me to be together.**"

I've heard many people smugly say that they would rather be in hell with all their friends than "sit around" in Heaven. As if the God who created relationships for the purpose of joy and happiness in the first place has no clue.

Ted Turner, the founder of CNN, had these remarks to say about Heaven when he spoke to the National Press Club a few years ago: "Remember, heaven is going to be perfect. And I don't really want to be there. Those of us that go to hell, which will be most of us in this room; most journalists are certainly going there. Who wants to go to a place that's perfect? Boring. Boring."

If people took the time to look into the nature of a loving God and what He really says in the Bible about how awesome and incredible our lives will be in Heaven, they wouldn't say such things. I like what C. S. Lewis had to say in *Mere Christianity* about people who misrepresent Heaven: "There is no need to be worried by facetious people who try to make the Christian hope of heaven ridiculous by saying they do not want to 'spend eternity playing harps.' The answer to such people is that if they cannot understand books written for grown-ups they should not talk about them."

40 Things You WON'T Find in Heaven

(20) Temptation

Waiting for the permanent Heaven

If a believer dies today, that person is in Paradise with Jesus. The current Heaven where our loved ones are now is more wonderful than they ever imagined. It's certainly more beautiful and inspiring than any place on earth. But as good at it is, the Bible tells us that God is going to create something even better. We read in Revelation 21 that God is going to create a new Heaven and a new earth. Just as He redeems and resurrects people, He will redeem and resurrect this old earth.

Probably the best book I've read about Heaven, besides the Bible, is Randy Alcorn's book entitled *Heaven*. And if you're looking for another great resource, I also recommend Dan Schaeffer's book entitled *A Better Country*. Randy Alcorn

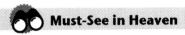

Must-See in Heaven

The Tree of Life

"The tree of life was on each side of the river, bearing twelve kinds of fruit, producing its fruit every month. The leaves of the tree are for healing the nations..." — **REVELATION 22:2** (csb)

describes the new creation this way: "It is no coincidence that the first two chapters of the Bible begin with the creation of the heavens and the earth and the last two chapters begin with the re-creation of the heavens and the earth. All that was lost at the beginning will be restored at the end—and far more will be added besides. The power of Christ's resurrection is enough not only to remake us, but also to remake every inch of the universe—mountains, rivers, plants, animals, stars, quasars, and galaxies."

So get ready for the most amazing new Heaven and new earth—more beautiful and bountiful than you can ever imagine. That's where we'll be living for eternity. And once you understand the things that we'll be doing in Heaven, you'll realize that there's no way it can be boring.

Yes, we will worship the King of Kings there. But that's not all. We'll be experiencing beauty in Heaven like never before. We'll be learning new things, like we did on earth, and exploring the expanse of the Heavenly realms. We'll be enjoying life as we did on earth but to an infinitely greater degree. We'll also be connecting with others on a level that wasn't entirely possible before because of flawed humanity's sin, pride, and selfishness.

What will all that be like? It will be, well, Heaven!

Enjoying incredible beauty and perfection

Stop for a moment and focus on your memory of the most beautiful place you've ever visited on this earth. I've sat on the edge of the Grand Canyon at sunrise, stood on the

shore of Lake Louise, Canada, and
golfed on the Monterey Peninsula
in California. I've felt the black
sands of Hawaii between my toes
and walked the warm beaches of
Fiji. But I'll never forget when my
daughters were young and we visited
Zion National Park in southern Utah. In the 1800s when
the Mormons were moving west, they came to this place of
majestic mountains, clear lakes, and rushing rivers. It was
so beautiful that they named it after Heaven—Zion. And for
all of my traveling, it is still probably the most breathtaking
location I've ever visited.

**40 Things
You WON'T
Find in Heaven**

㉑ Suicide

So where did you take your most beautiful Instagram and
Facebook pictures on vacation? Compared to the beauty of
the new Heaven and the new earth, even that is a garbage
dump.

Listen to how the apostle John described these future
destinations in Revelation 21:1-5: *"Then I saw 'a new
heaven and a new earth,' for the first heaven and the first
earth had passed away, and there was no longer any sea.
I saw the Holy City, the new Jerusalem, coming down
out of heaven from God, prepared as a bride beautifully
dressed for her husband. And I heard a loud voice from the
throne saying, 'Look! God's dwelling place is now among
the people, and he will dwell with them. They will be his
people, and God himself will be with them and be their
God. He will wipe every tear from their eyes. There will*

Travel Preview

★★★★★

No time, no days, no years, no death, no sickness...
just living with other believers and the King of
Kings!

TOM H.

be no more death or mourning or crying or pain, for the old order of things has passed away.' He who was seated on the throne said, 'I am making everything new!' Then he said, 'Write this down, for these words are trustworthy and true.'"

The apostle John was so overwhelmed by the beauty of the Holy City that he struggled to find a way to describe it. So he used a metaphor of a beautiful bride approaching her groom. I've performed hundreds of weddings, and I've never seen an ugly bride. Brides work for hours getting their hair, makeup, and dress just right. That's how John described the beauty of this celestial city—a bride on her wedding day.

Travel Tips

■ Take a refreshing dip in the River of Life and enjoy your new surroundings.

Feast your eyes on what the Bible says in Revelation 22:1-5 about the beautiful scenery in Heaven: *"Then the angel showed me the river of the water of life, as clear as crystal, flowing from the throne of God and of the Lamb down the middle of the great street of the city. On each side of the river stood the tree of life, bearing twelve crops of fruit, yielding its fruit every month. And the leaves of the tree are for the healing of the nations. No longer will there be any curse. The throne of God and of the Lamb will be in the city, and his servants will serve him. They will see his face, and his name will be on their foreheads. There will be no more night. They will not need the light of a lamp or the light of the sun, for the Lord God will give them light. And they will reign forever and ever."*

Just imagine walking down the main street of this stunning city. There is a pure, clear river gushing from God's throne down the middle of the avenue, and the sound of that rushing water as it flows beside you is mesmerizing. As you look up you see leafy trees lining both sides of the broad avenue. The Bible mentions "The Tree of Life" but that doesn't designate one tree—it identifies the *kind* of trees. It's like when people say, "The pine tree grows in East Texas." They aren't talking about a single tree, but a species of tree.

As you pass these rows of the Tree of Life, you discover they are fruit trees. The Bible says they produce a new crop of delicious fruit every month! The leaves of these trees have an unusual healing power—but we won't need to use them since we will never be sick. These are the leaves that were used from Heaven for the healing of the nations.

There won't be any need for streetlights because Heaven is in a new time zone. It's never night there. The Light of the Lord will illuminate the city. Whatever comes to mind when you picture this scene, the reality will certainly be beyond our wildest expectations!

Experiencing new things

Most of us enjoy new things—whether it's a new experience, a new car, a new gadget, or a new friend. The first Heaven and earth will dissolve like sugar crystals in a cup of hot tea, and the permanent Heaven will be full of new experiences. The Bible says that God will live among His people and be their God—that's new. God will also wipe away every tear. There will be no more reason to cry...no more death, heartache, or suffering. That will be a welcome new experience because this life is filled with all of those. There is so much that changes in the new Heaven that God just summarizes it from His throne and says, "I am making EVERYTHING new!"

40 Things You WON'T Find in Heaven

22 Funerals

Many earthly places have "new" in their names because they are named after "old" places. But they aren't necessarily improvements. I prefer the beautiful old city of York in England to the teeming mass of humanity living in "New" York. I've visited the lovely Jersey Island off the coast of France and consider it certainly prettier than "New" Jersey! The main feature of the new creation will be the Holy City of New Jerusalem. Currently, Jerusalem is a beautiful city. I love visiting there. But it won't compare to the NEW Jerusalem, which is another name used in the Bible for Heaven.

Exploring as never before

Many people live their whole lives dreaming of a vacation where they can do things they've never done before for a solid week or two. In Heaven you'll be able to do it every day of your life for eternity. I don't know exactly what this new earth will look like, but since it far exceeds the beauty of earth, I like to think we'll do things we never got to do here. For example, if you never experienced the thrill of climbing a mountain peak, I think you'll be able to do that in a heartbeat on a mountain more amazing than Kilimanjaro. If you never had a chance to walk the beautiful Camino de Santiago, you'll hike trails on the new earth that will make that famous hike in Spain seem like a walk to your mailbox. You'll be able to enjoy everything this new earth will have to offer and it will blow your mind.

But there's much more to the new Heaven and the new earth. And there's more than enjoying the Heavenly city. Look up—there are whole planets and galaxies that we'll be able to explore and we won't need a spacesuit to do it. Humanity has always had the urge to explore. That's why the Europeans sailed across the Atlantic in search for India and instead discovered what they called the New World. It's one of the reasons why the Pilgrims came over to America on the Mayflower. It's why Lewis and Clark set out for their expeditions from east to west. And it's why men and women looked up in the dark night sky at the moon and said, "I wonder what's it like up there."

40 Things You WON'T Find in Heaven

㉓ Anger

The 1960s was the decade of the space race with the Soviet Union. In eight years NASA went from putting a man in space to putting men on the moon. In 1968 movie producers extrapolated that same rate of scientific advancement and released the movie *2001: A Space Odyssey*. By 2001 we were supposed to have deep space vehicles capable of carrying humans to vast reaches of our solar system and beyond. Boy, were they wrong! At the time of this writing, we're not even sending space shuttles into orbit any more. We've sent a few space probes toward Mars and beyond, but we are basically an earthbound people.

The beginning lines of Star Trek are: "Space, the final frontier. These are the voyages of the starship *Enterprise*. Its continuing mission: to explore strange new worlds, to seek out new life and new civilizations, to boldly go where no one has gone before." Space isn't the final frontier. Heaven is. And we'll be able to explore it without a starship.

Dan Schaeffer writes: **"God has made us to explore and discover with great delight. We use spaceships and submarines because we need them, because our bodies are not perfectly fitted to explore our world without them. But Jesus, in His glorified body, which is the prototype of ours, was able to ignore the physical obstructions of our planet, like walls, gravity, density, and other things. Though physical Himself, He vanished and reappeared. He passed through solid walls. He floated up into heaven, defying gravity. Our new bodies will be made perfectly to explore the new heaven and earth. We have heard the phrase in history, 'the golden age of exploration.' In reality, that age lies ahead of us, not behind us."**

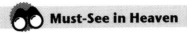

Must-See in Heaven

The 12 Jewels in the Foundations of the New Jerusalem

"The foundations of the city wall were adorned with every kind of jewel: the first foundation is jasper, the second sapphire, the third chalcedony, the fourth emerald, the fifth sardonyx, the sixth carnelian, the seventh chrysolite, the eighth beryl, the ninth topaz, the tenth chrysoprase, the eleventh jacinth, the twelfth amethyst."
— REVELATION 21:19-20 (csb)

Enjoying the animals

One of the questions I'm often asked is about animals. I think there will be all kinds of animals in Heaven. For example, we read in Revelation 19 that when Jesus returns for the final triumphant battle he will be riding a white horse. It seems to me that if there's a white horse, it's probable that there are other animals there.

But the wonderful thing about the animals in Heaven is that they will all be tame. There won't be animals of prey to fear or avoid. We know from Scripture that in the thousand-year reign of Christ on earth that animals will be peaceful and tame. Isaiah prophesied about this tame kingdom when he wrote, *"The wolf will dwell with the lamb, and the leopard will lie down with the goat. The calf, the young lion, and the fattened calf will be together, and a child will lead them. The cow and the bear will graze, their young ones will lie down together, and the lion will eat straw like cattle. An infant will play beside the cobra's pit, and a toddler will put his hand into a snake's den. They will not harm or destroy each other"* (Isaiah 11:6-9).

For many people, being separated from their pets is unthinkable. I understand that—and if I understand the happiness that people get from their pets in my limited human point of view, how much more will God account for that fact in Heaven?

Connecting with others

One of the best parts about Heaven is the heightened sense of connection we'll enjoy with other believers from every era of time. Imagine. You'll be with Moses *and* your roommate from college. With Ruth and Boaz *and* your favorite Sunday school teacher. And of course you'll be surrounded by the people you love. Let's explore some more of what our relationships in Heaven will be like in this next chapter.

CHAPTER 9

MAKING FRIENDS IN HEAVEN

One of the most enjoyable things about traveling is meeting people. As I have been fortunate to travel this planet, I have made many new friends. One of the greatest blessings of visiting foreign countries is meeting the people who live there. For instance, a few years ago I was invited to visit the tiny chain of islands in the South Pacific that form the country of Fiji. I traveled there with a small group to train pastors and to help provide some much-needed disaster relief from a recent typhoon that had destroyed much of the main island. After a long overnight flight, we landed in the early morning hours at Fiji's international airport in Nadi.

We were exhausted as we walked off the plane. But our hearts were refreshed when we saw eight or nine Fijian Christians standing in a line, singing us a welcome song. The women were dressed in their local attire and placed a necklace around our necks and a kiss on our cheeks. Suddenly we were no longer tired. We were energized. These brothers and sisters in Christ became our instant friends even though we had never met them before. And I am still in contact with some of them.

Welcome to Heaven

In the same way we will enjoy an instant bond in Heaven with people we've never met before. Our welcome in Heaven will be a thrilling experience. Here's how John described the people he saw in Heaven: *"After this I looked, and there before me was a great multitude that no one could count, from every nation, tribe, people and language, standing before the throne and before the Lamb. They were wearing white robes and were holding palm branches in their hands"* (Revelation 7:9).

This doesn't mean that we'll always be wearing white robes and waving palm branches. Revelation 7 is describing a specific coronation event in Heaven. But notice the multitude— people from every nation, tribe, and language. These will be our forever friends and fellow citizens of Heaven.

You'll have a chance to ask King David how big Goliath really was. You'll meet a tall tax collector named Zacchaeus. And as one of my Facebook friends posted, you'll meet Eve and Sarah and be able to ask them, "What were you *thinking*?" You'll be able to ask Daniel what it was like to spend the night reading between the lions. (Sorry.)

You can ask Moses what it was like to walk through the Red Sea without getting his sandals wet. You can ask Solomon what it was like to have a thousand mothers-in-law! You can ask Noah what it was like to spend 40 days on a huge boat with an entire zoo onboard. You may think that you'll ask Peter what it was like to walk·on water, but in Heaven, that won't be a challenge any more.

And there won't just be famous Bible characters in Heaven. All the wonderful saints who have lived and died throughout the ages will be there to befriend as well. Personally, I can't

---

Travel Preview

⭐⭐⭐⭐⭐

I'm looking forward to meeting my birth mother who died after giving me birth.

MARLA S.

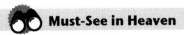 **Must-See in Heaven**

David

Ask him how big Goliath really was.

wait to trade "preacher stories" with John Wesley, Jonathan Edwards, and Charles Spurgeon. I also want to have a long talk with Eric Liddell about what winning that Olympic gold medal and then devoting the rest of his life to be a missionary. I want to ask Jim Elliot, Nate Saint, Ed McCully, Peter Fleming, and Roger Youderian to describe their encounter with the Huaorani people in the jungles of Ecuador. As the natives attacked them, they valiantly refused to use their firearms to defend themselves because those young men knew where they would be if they died—and they didn't want to take away the opportunity for their killers to know Christ also one day. It's going to be so cool to meet some of those tribesmen who killed the missionaries and later became believers!

Will I know my family members? Will they know me?

The most frequent question I've been asked about Heaven is, "Will we know our family members there?" Absolutely. You'll know them better than you ever knew them in this life. The Bible says in 1 Corinthians that you will *"know even as you are known."*

One of my best friends growing up was named Andy. We usually walked home from school together and there was a place where the sidewalk divided to go around a huge tree. As we passed on different sides of that old tree, we had a funny tradition. I would say, "Needles" and he would respond, "Pins." Then he would say, "Bread" and I would say, "Butter." I can't remember why we said that—maybe we thought it was for good luck. But we must have said it a thousand times. We played sports on the same team and sang in the youth choir together. I haven't seen Andy in many years, but I expect to know him in Heaven. And as we walk around one of the many trees, I'm sure we'll remember to say, "Needles and Pins" and "Bread and Butter."

40 Things You WON'T Find in Heaven

㉔ Hunger

We have plenty of evidence from the Bible that after a person of faith died, they didn't lose a distinct identity. At the Transfiguration of Jesus, two Old Testament saints appeared and talked with Jesus—Elijah and Moses. They each maintained a distinct appearance because the disciples saw them and identified them. So yes, I'll know Andy right away. And yes, you will know your loved ones in Heaven.

If your great-great grandparents knew Jesus, you'll get to know them. Won't it be fun to swap stories with them? They won't seem old to you and you won't seem young to them. And that precious baby who died in the womb or as a newborn? Absolutely. You'll know him or her in the fullness of their potential for vitality.

Jesus took children in His arms and received them and blessed them. He's still doing that. When King David's infant son died he said, *"He cannot return to me; but I can go to him"* (2 Samuel 12:23). David believed that his son was in a good place where David would meet him someday in the future. According to Hebrews 11, David is in Heaven, so we can know that's where he joined his son. Your loved ones will be closer to you than they ever were on earth.

But here's the thing. You'll know EVERYONE in Heaven better than you know your closest friends and family members now. Usually we reserve our closest relationships for family and a few close friends. Can you imagine what it will be like to truly know and love all the redeemed of all the ages?

The most amazing people you'll ever meet

In this life we only get to know a few people on a deep, personal level. I've often wished that I could know everyone I meet on that deep level. But there's something in our human personality that wants to guard our innermost thoughts. In this life we all have a sin-influenced heart that drives us isolate ourselves. We're shy and withdrawn because we're afraid of hurting people or of being hurt.

And in this life, there are multitudes of annoying, obnoxious people who also happen to be Christians. I may be a pastor, but I am not blind to the offenses of others! We don't really want to get to know that kind of person better, do we? The thought of spending eternity with them may even give us the willies. But imagine when that person is transformed to be like Jesus and so are you. C. S. Lewis wrote that **"the dullest and most uninteresting person you can talk to may one day be a creature which, if you saw it now, you would be strongly tempted to worship."**

Dan Schaeffer adds: **"Heaven will be a city of new people— regenerated, renewed, and perfect. Imagine upon arriving in heaven that you discovered to your delight, that the first person you met loved you so dearly and deeply that it fairly took your breath away and that this expression of love neither embarrassed you nor made you feel strange. You were able to receive this person's love as easily as he or she was able to give it.** Then imagine the next person you met loved you with an equivalent, but unique, perfect love as well."**

Travel Tips

■ You won't need to keep up with your keys in Heaven—the gates are never locked. (Revelation 21:25)

Have you ever met a celebrity or sports star? Do you remember how excited you were to meet him or her and maybe have your picture taken? A friend told me once that he drove all the way to Houston to meet George W. Bush. And instead of shaking hands, President Bush embraced him in a bear hug. Wow! Just imagine that kind of thrill upon meeting every person in Heaven.

When you think about it, however, you shouldn't wait to arrive in Heaven to have deep relationships. Knowing what kind of friendships we will have in Heaven should motivate

Travel Preview

⭐⭐⭐⭐⭐

In Heaven, there will be nothing to fear...totally void of hate and injustice. Only pure love, peace, kindness, joy, and serenity.

SAM T.

all of us to be more loving and kind to all people here and now. God gives us instructions on how to LOVE, truly LOVE, people. The Bible says we are to bear their burdens and love them as ourselves. Earth is training school for Heaven where we'll finally be able to love like Jesus taught us to do.

That love doesn't stop once the person dies, by the way. You will get a chance to love your family and friends better than you were ever able to do consistently on earth. You will connect with them in ways you always desired to do but something held you back. Our fallen nature created protective barriers that won't exist in Heaven. ALL relationships will be deepened in Heaven, including the relationship with your spouse.

Will we be married in Heaven?

This brings us to another question I've been asked about Heaven. Will we be married in Heaven? What about a person who has been married several times? Who will be his or her mate? This is a question that's at least 2,000 years old. The enemies of Jesus asked Him a crooked question about marriage in Heaven and Jesus gave a straight answer. He said, *"Are you not in error because you do not know the scriptures or the power of God? When the dead rise, they will neither marry nor be given in marriage; they will be like the angels in heaven"* (Mark 12:24-25).

As I wrote earlier, Jesus didn't say we would BE angels. He said that we would be LIKE the angels. In this context He points out that angels don't get married. What did He mean by that? He was teaching us at least two things. One, there will be no NEW marriages in Heaven. But He didn't mean that the institution of marriage would be dissolved. Contrary to what some people believe, we will be married in Heaven. We'll be married

40 Things You WON'T Find in Heaven

㉕ Thirst

to Jesus because the Bible teaches that the Church is the Bride of Christ.

Remember what I said about earth being a school to prepare us for Heaven? The human relationship of marriage is for our enjoyment, but ultimately its purpose is to teach us about the love relationship between Christ and His Church. That's why the Bible says for husbands to love their wives like Jesus loves the Church (Ephesians 5:25).

Dan Schaeffer writes, **"In heaven, in His presence forever, we will finally eat the banquet for which all human marriages and loves were but hors d'oeuvres. We will not miss having the one human relationship through which we find our life and fulfillment, for we shall finally experience the real thing with our Lord."**

Every human relationship will be overshadowed by our relationship with God. Think of it this way. If you are a Christian couple, you feel a certain bond with your husband or wife. When you pray together, that bond becomes even stronger. Now imagine a spiritual bond a million times more powerful—that's the bond you'll have with your first love, Jesus.

You may be single, widowed, or divorced. But in Heaven all previous relationships will be outweighed by the unparalleled love relationship with Jesus. When you see Jesus face to face, your deepest yearning for acceptance and intimacy will finally be totally fulfilled. And you will be overjoyed to see that the person you loved the most on earth will experience the same thing.

What else will we DO in Heaven?

High on the list of Heaven's activity guide is music and worship. But I promise you—Heaven isn't going to be 6,000 verses of the same praise chorus. It's not going to be a sermon that lasts 40 years either. Instead the most amazing praise and worship will comprise the very atmosphere of Heaven, and it will be music to your ears.

 Must-See in Heaven

The 12 Foundations of the New Jerusalem

"The city wall had twelve foundations, and the twelve names of the twelve apostles of the Lamb were on the foundations."
—REVELATION 21:14 (csb)

CHAPTER 10

THE SOUNDTRACK OF HEAVEN

Some of you plan special evenings out to enjoy concerts, operas, and musicals. When you travel, you might enjoy looking in the paper or online to see who is playing in town. Or you might book a special restaurant that offers live music while you dine. Music is a big part of your life and you look forward to these events as an essential part of your entertainment and joy. Your own the soundtrack to your favorite movies, you pay attention to the background music being played in elevators and grocery stores, and your favorite part of a church service is the worship. If any of this resonates with you, you're getting just a taste of what the future will be like in Heaven.

The Bible explains that we will be engulfed in a beautiful symphony of praise in Heaven. When John arrived in Heaven there was a specific scene of worship taking place. Pay attention to what he says because you'll experience this yourself one day. He wrote: *"I saw a Lamb, looking as if it had been slain...Then I looked and heard the voice of many angels, numbering thousands upon thousands, and ten thousand times ten thousand. They encircled the throne and the living creatures and the elders. In a loud voice they were saying: 'Worthy is the Lamb, who was slain, to receive power and wealth and wisdom and strength and honor and glory and praise!'"* (Revelation 5:6, 11-12)

This is a specific event described more in detail in Revelation 5:8 where the Lamb of God, Jesus, comes forward and opens a scroll to announce the final chapter of this world's drama. It takes place in the throne room of Heaven as saints (that's us) and angels gather around the throne. A mighty angel asks if anyone is worthy to open a special scroll. But no one steps forward immediately.

In Bible times scrolls were often used to record deeds and official details of an inheritance—like our modern last will and testament. So what is this Heavenly scroll? It's more than a piece of paper. It is symbolic, for it represents our forfeited inheritance to Paradise. Think of it as the title deed to all that the first man God created, Adam, forfeited when he sinned in the Garden of Eden.

To put it in Hebrew real estate language, the angel was looking for a kinsman. When someone was at risk of losing property, only a legal kinsman could buy it back. Only a family member could pay the price to redeem the inheritance. Jesus Christ was a part of the family of man because He was like us in every way. Since He qualified as a kinsman, He paid the precious price of His blood on the cross to purchase back our access to all that was lost in Paradise. The Bible says, *"For you know that you were redeemed from your empty way of life inherited from your fathers, not with perishable things like silver or gold, but with the precious blood of Christ, like that of an unblemished and spotless lamb"* (1 Peter 1:18-19).

After the angel asks who is worthy to open the scroll and there is no response, John begins to weep because all seems lost. But then one of the elders says, *"Don't weep! See the Lion of the Tribe of Judah, the Root of David, has triumphed. He is able to open the scroll!"* (Revelation 5:5)

John looks up with tears in his eyes and sees a Lamb "appearing to be slain," though the Lamb is standing. This of course, is Jesus, the sacrificial Lamb of God *and* the triumphant Lion of the Tribe of Judah. He steps forward to take the scroll and when he does ... THE CROWD GOES

WILD! The angels and saints break out in a symphony of worship and praise.

We'll be there. Even the most powerful worship services we've ever experienced on earth are *nothing* compared to what this inaugural experience will be like in Heaven! We'll be celebrating Jesus from that day forward.

Travel Preview

★★★★★

Heaven is going to be far beyond anything we can imagine! Going from decay and death to stunningly brilliant colors and amazing new bodies...woo hoo! When I was a child, a friend of the family's young son died. My brothers took it hard until someone told them that their friend was skateboarding on streets made of gold. I always liked that imagery.

KIM B.

Worship that WOWS

I've been preaching for around 50 years, and there has never been a Sunday morning when I woke up and said, "Oh no, it's Sunday again." I love Sundays! But I realize that most people can't take too much church. It's funny, but the most enjoyable thing a lot of people do at church is to LEAVE! Worship is over, and they storm out to get to their cars and head home or out to lunch. Some of the really adept church leavers park in such a way to make the fastest getaway. It's as if they think, "Okay. I've put in my time for the week. I'm good until next Sunday." No wonder the mistaken idea of Heaven being an eternal church service isn't that appealing to most folks.

John Eldridge confesses this idea in his book *The Journey of Desire*: "We have settled on an image of the never-ending sing-along in the sky; one great hymn after another, forever and ever, amen. And our heart sinks. Forever and ever? That's it? That's the good news? And then we sigh and feel guilty that we are not more 'spiritual.' We lose heart, and we turn once more to the present to find what life we can."

I think praise in Heaven will be more like the soundtrack of a great movie. The music is there, but

㉖ Cell Phones

you're not really aware of it except that it is moving you and enhancing your enjoyment of the experience. I listen to relaxing music whenever I study and write. Just as you listen to the radio or your digital device when you're driving or working, the Heavenly symphony of praise will surround you.

I love attending worship services with other believers, especially in other cultures. Some people call it "going to church." But I always remind people: You don't GO to church; you ARE the church! I love singing songs of praise and I love teaching and hearing the Word of God taught. I've worshipped in Lutheran churches in Germany where they sang stiffly, but with great enthusiasm, the great hymns such as "A Mighty Fortress Is Our God." I've been in downtown Beijing on a Sunday morning and heard believers sing passionate songs of praise in Mandarin and I only understood two words: *Alleluia* and *Amen*.

I've been on remote islands in the Philippines and watched believers worship with tears of joy streaming down their faces. And I've been in dirt-floored gatherings in Africa where the believers can sing and dance praising Jesus for hours

 Must-See in Heaven

A Multitude of Angels

"Then I looked and heard the voice of many angels around the throne, and also of the living creatures and of the elders. Their number was countless thousands, plus thousands of thousands."
—REVELATION 5:11 (CSB)

without a break. They literally raise a cloud of dust from the floor that is as beautiful as the incense in the Jewish Temple. God loves all kinds of music and expressions of worship, as long as it comes from the heart.

What I'm saying is that the music of Heaven will have an international dimension to it because the Bible says people from every tribe and tongue will be there praising Jesus (Revelation 7:9). Think of it. You'll be side by side with brothers and sisters in Christ from every country on earth—and from every era of time—who will be praising God alongside you. I can hardly wait!

Singing like Jesus

My mother was a wonderful Christian who taught me about Jesus from an early age. But she didn't have any musical ability. I can remember standing next to her in church and hearing her sing. She was awful! She could carry a tune; she just couldn't unload it. I jokingly say that my mom was what some people call "a prisoner singer." That's someone who is always behind a few bars and can't find the right key!

As a teen I was embarrassed to stand beside her in church. In fact I used to tell her not to sing. But she didn't listen to me. She would still make a joyful noise—emphasis on noise. Today I realize how selfish I was in asking her not to sing. Today I cherish the memory of her singing. She's in Heaven now, and just as we will do one day, she is singing along with the choir of Heaven in a beautiful voice. If I had any sense as a kid, I would have told my mom, "Sing, Mom! Sing!" I'll just have to make up for it one day when we stand next to each other in Heaven again singing to the Lord.

In Heaven, since we'll be like Jesus, we'll be able to sing like Jesus. Many people are surprised to learn that Jesus is a singer. The Bible says, *"So Jesus is not ashamed to call them brothers. He says, 'I will declare your name to my brothers; in the presence of the congregation I will sing your praises'"* (Hebrews 2:12). This verse refers to

Jesus fulfilling Psalm 22:22 where Jesus is speaking in the first person: *"I will declare your name [God's name] to my brothers; in the presence of the congregation I will sing your praises."*

Did you know that we have a singing Savior? Maybe you've never thought about it. Jesus sang during His earthly ministry, and according to Hebrews 2, He's STILL singing! Both Matthew and Mark write how after the Last Supper Jesus and the disciples sang a hymn and went to the Mount of Olives. What did they sing? The psalm usually sung after the Passover meal was Psalm 118. The Jews still sing it after their Passover meal today.

40 Things You WON'T Find in Heaven

(27) Credit Cards

So just imagine that you're there in the Upper Room. Jesus knows that He is headed to Gethsemane to be arrested, tortured, and eventually crucified. Listen as they sing these words: *"Give thanks to the Lord, for he is good; his love endures forever. The Lord is with me; I will not be afraid. What can mere mortals do to me? The Lord is with me; he is my helper. Shouts of joy and victory resound in the tents of the righteous: 'The Lord's right hand has done mighty things!' I will not die but live, and will proclaim what the Lord has done. The Lord is my strength and my defense; he has become my salvation. The stone the builders rejected has become the cornerstone; the Lord has done this, and*

Travel Preview

LAURA H.

My favorite thought of Heaven was given to me by my father while he was in the hospital. He said, "The first thing I'm going to do when I get to Heaven is crawl up in my Father's lap." I've never felt such peace as when I realized what a comfort that would be.

it is marvelous in our eyes. The Lord has done it this very day; let us rejoice today and be glad!"

God invented music. He loves to be praised. The Lord Himself is the sweet singer of salvation. The prophet Zephaniah described Him singing over His people: *"The Lord your God is with you, the Mighty Warrior who saves. He will take great delight in you; in his love he will no longer rebuke you, but will rejoice over you with singing"* (Zephaniah 3:17).

Staying in tune forever

What I'm saying is don't worry if you can't sing now. Go ahead and make a joyful noise unto the Lord. And smile when you anticipate the day when you'll be engulfed in a symphony of praise in Heaven. What will make us break out in song? When you are up close and personal with Jesus. You'll read about that climactic Heavenly scene in the next chapter.

 **Must-See in Heaven**

The Supernatural Source of Light

"The city does not need the sun or the moon to shine on it, because the glory of God illuminates it, and its lamp is the Lamb."
— REVELATION 21:23 (csb)

CHAPTER 11

MEETING THE KING

Red Square is a huge open area framed by the Kremlin and the beautiful onion-domed St. Basil's Cathedral. When I saw it the first time I was amazed at the size. The Russians claim that it is the largest public square in the world. Every day tens of thousands of people line up to file into a building in front of the Kremlin that has the appearance of a shrine. It is Lenin's mausoleum. The people wait for hours in all kinds of weather just to walk by and get a glimpse of the preserved body of Lenin.

I've also had the opportunity to visit Tiananmen Square in Beijing, where the Chinese also claim to have the largest public square in the world! On the west side of the square one can see the massive Great Hall of the People where the Communist Party meets. At the north end is the mysterious Forbidden City, the ancient palace of the Chinese emperors. The mausoleum of Mao Zedong dominates the center of the square. When Mao died in 1975 he left instructions for his body to be cremated, but his followers ignored his desires and had his body embalmed and encased in a crystal coffin. Then they built the mausoleum to preserve his legacy. Every day of the year in China, as many as 17,000 people queue up to wait for hours on end to walk by and see the remains of the corpse of Mao Zedong for a few seconds.

Frankly, I don't like standing in long lines to do anything.

And that must be why I always seem to pick the slowest line no matter what I do! God is working on my character and teaching me patience. It's so bad that I tell people that if they see me in line at the grocery store, don't get in line behind me

40 Things You WON'T Find in Heaven

(28) Debt Collectors

because I will inevitably be behind the person whose credit card doesn't work, or who wants to go back and get another item, or who takes the time to write a check!

You realize that there will be millions of saints in Heaven. Won't there be long lines to see Jesus, the main attraction? Nope. Think about it. Today when I pray, I have immediate access to God. I don't have to get in a line to offer my prayers and petitions. God can hear and answer billions of prayers simultaneously. Our access in Heaven will be even better. Remember, God is omnipresent and Jesus is God, so He will still be ever-present and available to you.

I agree with Dan Schaeffer, who wrote, **"I believe that when we enter eternal life the angels will take us to our Lord for a private audience, and over eternity, we will experience unlimited private audiences with the Lord. Finally I won't have to wonder what He is thinking or wanting from me. I will know for He will tell me. Personally. Privately. Intimately."**

Face to Face

I heard a funny story about a Sunday school teacher who was teaching her class of children about Heaven. She wanted them to understand the importance of believing in Jesus so she asked them, "Now, boys and girls, what do you have to do to go to Heaven?" One little boy shot his hand up and said, "You have to DIE!" That was a downer to her lesson, but the little boy was correct nonetheless.

One second we may be looking in the face of a loved one, our favorite dog, or a friend at lunch, and the next second we could be looking into the face of Jesus because we will have left this earth. We never know when we may die or be raptured, so we should always stay ready to meet Jesus.

When it's your time to die and you've taken your last look in the faces of the ones you loved on earth, in the next moment you will finally see the face of the One who loves you more than anyone has ever loved you. He alone has been thinking of you every moment of every day from the moment you were born. The Bible says, *"They will see his face, and his name will be on their foreheads"* (Revelation 22:4). That doesn't mean that His name will be tattooed on our heads! It means that He will always be foremost in our minds and thoughts.

Paul wrote, *"For now we see in a mirror dimly, but then face to face"* (1 Corinthians 13:12). The language Paul uses is of a blurred image, like looking at a picture that's out of focus. Or like trying to see your face in a mirror that's all fogged up. You can see something, but it's not clear. Those of us who love Jesus are always looking for His face. We see it dimly now with our eyes of faith. But one day we'll look straight at Jesus. Five hundred years ago John Donne wrote: **"No man ever saw God and lived. And yet, I shall not live till I see God."** We haven't really lived until we've died and seen the lover of our souls! This is what Randy Alcorn meant when he wrote, **"The day I die will be the best day I've ever lived."**

Fanny Crosby was a prolific hymn writer. She wrote such classic songs as "Blessed Assurance" and "To God Be the Glory." Fanny Crosby was blind, so she possessed a keen anticipation of being able to see once she died. In one of her songs she wrote, **"When my life work is ended, and I cross**

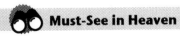 **Must-See in Heaven**

Spot all 12 names of the apostles on the 12 foundations

"The city wall had twelve foundations, and the twelve names of the twelve apostles of the Lamb were on the foundations."
— REVELATION 21:14 (csb)

the swelling tide, When the bright and glorious morning I shall see; I shall know my Redeemer when I reach the other side, And His smile will be the first to welcome me."

Travel Preview

⭐⭐⭐⭐⭐

My parents, husband, and sons beat me to Heaven's door. So to me, Heaven is a wonderful place where you can feel right at home the moment you arrive.

LIZZIE MAE B.

What should I do when I see Jesus?

Some people imagine that when they first see Jesus that they will run up to Him and give Him a high-five or fist bump. There was a time when I thought my first meeting with Jesus would be like that old shampoo commercial—the one where two people are in a beautiful field running toward each other in slow motion. Music is playing and their freshly shampooed hair is bouncing gently. Then finally they meet each other in an embrace and spin around slowly as the music crescendos.

Since then as I've studied God's Word, I have dropped that mental image. There's a popular Christian song about imagining what we'll do when we see Jesus. I don't think that we'll dance. I don't think that we'll jump for joy. I believe that we'll do exactly the same thing that John did when he encountered the risen Christ. He had hung around Jesus during His earthly ministry for three years, eating and drinking and talking to each other as friends. But the Bible says that John *"fell down at his feet like a dead man"* (Revelation 1:17) when He saw the glorified Jesus. John was so overwhelmed by the sight and voice of Jesus in His resurrected state that he fainted.

I believe we will all fall at the feet of Jesus when we see Him in all of His majesty and glory. But I believe Jesus will respond in compassion to each of us just as He did John. John wrote, *"He laid his right hand on me and said, 'Don't be afraid. I am the First and the Last, and the Living One. I was dead, but look—I am alive forever and ever'"* (Revelation 1:17-18).

40 Things You WON'T Find in Heaven

(29) Pushy Salespersons

Will Jesus judge me in Heaven?

There are very few scenes described for us in Heaven, as far as a daily itinerary like you would have on a planned vacation. But there are a few. One scene we discussed in the last chapter takes place when the Lamb appears to open the scroll and all of Heaven erupts in praise. If you're a Christian, you will be there for that.

There is another scene that will take place in Heaven called The Judgment Seat of Christ. The Bible says, *"For we must all appear before the judgment seat of Christ, so that each of us may receive what is due us for the things done while in the body, whether good or bad"* (2 Corinthians 5:10).

I remember there was a popular Christian movie out in the Eighties about a high school student who goes to Heaven and sees a gigantic card catalog. Remember those from libraries? He pulls out a drawer and inside is card after card describing every sin he'd ever committed. It's embarrassing to the core. There are also renditions of this scene where everything you've ever done wrong is played on a 1,152-inch screen in Heaven in high definition for all your loved ones and perfect strangers to see as you cringe at the revelation of all your dirty laundry.

Is that going to happen in Heaven? No, you can be sure it won't be that way.

There is widespread confusion among Christians about this. I think some well-meaning pastors have even preached this errant philosophy as a means to try to get Christians to behave! There will be a judgment. But this judgment will NOT be a place where we will answer for our sins—our sins were dealt with at the cross. Romans 8:1 assures us, *"There is now no condemnation for those who are in Christ Jesus."*

The idea we will have to pay for our deeds at the judgment seat is totally false—the debt for our sins was already paid at the cross.

So what is this judgment about?

The word translated "judgment seat" in this passage is the Greek word *bema*. It is best translated as "stage" or "platform." A bema was a raised platform where rulings and rewards were publicly announced. When we toured the ruins of ancient Corinth we saw the remains of the bema in Corinth. This is where minor rulings were made, but mostly it was where they would pass out the awards to the winners of athletic contests. The chief official or judge sat on the bema so he could see the competition and make a fair determination of the winner who was summoned to the bema to receive his reward.

Are you getting the picture yet? Jesus will be on the bema in Heaven, and we'll be summoned to receive our prize.

In order to clear up another element of confusion about the judgment day mentioned in 2 Corinthians, it's important for you

40 Things You WON'T Find in Heaven

(30) Gossip

to know that this judgment IS NOT the judgment Jesus spoke about in Matthew 25. That's another scene that takes place in Heaven when Jesus will separate the sheep from the goats. It's also called the judgment of the nations. NOR is this the Great White Throne Judgment mentioned in Revelation 20. That's yet another scene described for us in Scripture where all the lost from all the ages will be cast into the lake of fire that is the second death.

In 1 Corinthians 3:10-15, Paul gives us some more helpful details about what will happen at the judgment seat of Christ: *"But each one should be careful how he builds. For no one can lay any foundation other than the one already laid, which is Jesus Christ. If any man builds on this foundation using gold, silver, costly stones, wood, hay or straw, his work will be shown for what it is, because the Day will bring it to light. It will be revealed with fire, and the fire will test the quality of each man's work. If what he has built survives, he will receive his reward. If it is burned up, he will suffer loss; he himself will be saved, but only as one escaping through the flames."*

> **Travel Tips**
>
> ■ Don't miss the Heavenly River Walk. Feel free to walk down either side of the River of Life flowing down the main street of Heaven. (Revelation 22:2)

In order to help you understand exactly what will take place, let me answer a few questions about this Heavenly scene.

Who will be at the judgment?

This answer is short and simple: only Christians will be there, and ALL Christians will be there. When Paul wrote "we must all appear," he was referring to all Christians. Most conservative theologians believe this will be an experience only for the Church—the Bride of Christ. We won't be the only ones who spend eternity with Jesus in Heaven. There will also be Old Testament saints and Tribulation saints. The Old Testament saints, like Abraham and Moses, and the Tribulation saints, those who refuse to bear the mark of the beast during the future tribulation, will go through a similar judgment after the seven-year tribulation. (See Daniel 12:1-2; Matthew 8:11; Revelation 20:4-6.)

Judge Jesus will be there. His knowledge is perfect and His evaluation is flawless. We won't judge ourselves, because most of us have major blind spots. We won't be judged by our friends and family because they might be too lenient. We won't be judged by our enemies because they might want to kick us out of Heaven altogether. There won't be a chance for people to call in and vote for us. You won't vote for me and I won't vote for you—we'll all be judged by the perfect judge, Judge Jesus.

Where, when, and what will happen?

This will take place in Heaven after the Rapture and before Christ returns to set up His Kingdom on earth. Jesus often spoke about being rewarded in Heaven. For instance he said, ***"Rejoice and be glad, because great is your reward in heaven"*** (Matthew 5:12). He will be evaluating each of us on the basis of what we did with what He gave us. We've been given gifts and abilities, and on that day, we'll be judged according to our stewardship of His gifts.

There are two main things that will happen:

(1) It will be a time of revelation of the quality of my service to God.

We read in 1 Corinthians 3:13, ***"It will be revealed with fire, and the fire will test the quality of each man's work."*** Notice it's the QUALITY of each person's work—not the quantity—that's at stake. The Bible uses the metaphor of building a house. The foundation is Jesus Christ. Once Jesus is the foundation of my life, then I start building a superstructure of Christian service upon that foundation. The Bible mentions six kinds of building materials: gold, silver, jewels, wood, hay, and straw.

But those six materials are divided into two broad groups. Gold, silver, and jewels are precious, permanent materials. They represent all the things we do for Jesus in the power of the Spirit and for the glory of God alone. Wood, hay, and straw are cheaper, perishable materials. They represent all of the Christian service we perform in our own strength and with a desire for people to recognize how good WE are—in other words, we do it for our own glory.

So when we stand at the bema, each of us will present a

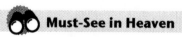

Must-See in Heaven

Daniel

Ask him what it was like to spend the night with lions.

building that we've built through our Christian service. Then Jesus will look at our building of works and it will ignite—the quality of our work will be tried by fire. Remember, in Revelation 1:14, John had a vision of the glorified Christ and John wrote that Jesus' eyes were like a blazing fire. When Jesus gazes at my works, it will be like a laser beam—poof! My life's work will burst into flame.

What happens to gold, silver, and jewels when they go through fire? They aren't destroyed, they are simply purified—and they remain. So everything I've done in the power of the Spirit and for the glory of God will just be more beautiful and precious for Jesus. But when wood, hay, and straw catches fire, not much is left over. Everything I've ever done to receive the attention or praise of others will go up in smoke. Oh, the foundation will remain, but the straw house will be gone.

(2) It will also be a time of reward for the faithfulness of my service to God.

After the quality of our service is tried by fire the Bible says, "If what he has built survives, he will receive his reward." In Matthew 25 Jesus told a story about a business owner who left for an extended trip. He left three of his employees in charge. To one the owner gave $5,000, to another he gave $2,000, and to the third he gave $1,000—according to their abilities. In my rendition of the story, the owner said, "Go to work, and see what you can do with that capital."

After a long absence the owner returned and the employee with $5,000 said, "Sir, I've doubled it—here's $10,000 for you." The owner said, "Great job! Keep it—you're now my partner." The second employee said, "Sir, I've doubled your money—here's $4,000." The owner said, "Great job! Keep it—you're my partner now." The third employee came forward and said, "Sir, I know how tight-fisted you are and how you hate to lose money, so I put the $1,000 in a mayonnaise jar and buried it in my backyard. Here's all your money back—$1,000." The owner frowned and said, "What? You mean you didn't even buy a Certificate of Deposit, or put it in an interest-bearing checking account? You're not only lazy, you're wicked—and my money smells like mayonnaise—you're fired."

Do you see the point of the story? We will receive what is due us for the things we did in this body—whether good or bad. The "bad" deeds aren't sins like lying or stealing, but poor stewardship. God has given me gifts and abilities. I will be rewarded on the basis of how faithful I've been to use these gifts for the glory of God. Every Christian is a minister—you have God-given gifts and abilities too. If you are a Christian who isn't serving God, it's like hiding the Master's investment in a stinky mayonnaise jar! Remember that to whom much is given, much is required (Luke 12:48).

So this judgment isn't about salvation or sin; it's all about your service. It's not a time of condemnation; it's a time of commendation. It's not a time of punishment, but a time of praise. It's not a time of rebuke, but a time of reward.

How will we react?

According to the words we read in 2 Corinthians 5 and 1 Corinthians 3, there will basically be two different reactions on that day.

For some, it will be a time of rejoicing. In the parable of the talents, the master says to his faithful servants, "Well done, good and faithful servant, enter into the JOY of your salvation." As Paul was approaching his death he was looking forward to the bema. He wrote, ***"Now there is in store for me the crown of righteousness, which the Lord, the righteous Judge, will award to me on that day—and not only to me, but also to all who have longed for his appearing"*** (2 Timothy 4:8). Paul wrote that he was looking forward to seeing Jesus because he expected to receive a crown of righteousness. The reward we receive at the bema comes in the form of crowns. There are two words for "crowns" in the New Testament. One is *diadema*, which means a royal crown. The other is *stephanos*, which means a garland crown—the kind that was given to runners who had finished the race. So which of those two do you think we'll receive? Right.

Only Jesus will wear a *diadema* (Revelation 14:14).

The New Testament mentions at least five different kinds of crowns—a crown of righteousness, a crown of life, a crown of rejoicing, a crown of glory, and a victor's crown. If you want to study more about those, just get a concordance and trace the word "crown" in the New Testament. On that day when Jesus passes out crowns, there will be great rejoicing in Heaven. Have you ever been at an award ceremony? There is a sense of excitement and anticipation, and when the emcee announces the winner of an award, there is spontaneous applause. I think that's going to be the scene at the bema. There are certain people I want to stand around when Jesus starts passing out the crowns because I want to rejoice in the celebration.

In Matthew 6 Jesus spoke about those people who pray for public recognition and do works for the applause of men—He says that's ALL the reward they'll get—man's applause. But in Matthew 6:6 He says of those who fast, serve, and pray in secret, **"Your Father who sees in secret will REWARD you openly."** Sometimes people have to perform acts of love and service called "thankless jobs." Maybe you've had to take care of a dying loved one whose body has regressed to that of a helpless baby. Maybe you've had to live with your mother-in-law! Remember, there is no thankless job. Your thanks and reward will come later—it will come from Jesus Himself!

For others, it will be a time of regret. The Bible speaks of that individual whose work is composed primarily of wood, hay, and straw. Much of what they did was for show, and with a desire for recognition and credit. Eugene Petersen paraphrases it this way: *"Eventually there is going to be an inspection. If you use cheap or inferior materials, you'll be found out. The inspection will be thorough and rigorous. You won't get by with a thing. If your work passes inspection, fine; if it doesn't, your part of the building will be torn out and started over. But you won't be torn out; you'll survive—but just barely"* (1 Corinthians 3:10, MSG). John Greenleaf Whittier wrote, "Of all sad words of tongue or pen, the saddest are these, 'It might have been.'" I really don't want to stand before Jesus and watch my service burn up into a pile of ashes. The thought of the bema motivates me to serve the Lord more faithfully and more humbly than ever before.

But I don't need any crowns...

Will we be walking around Heaven all day with crowns on our heads? No. The Bible says that after we receive our crowns, we're going to take them off and lay them before the feet of Jesus. *"The twenty-four elders* [that's us] *fall down before him who sits on the throne, and worship him who lives for ever and ever. They lay their crowns before the throne and say: 'You are worthy, our Lord and God, to receive glory and honor and power, for you created all things, and by your will they were created and have their being'"* (Revelation 4:10-11).

Through the years, when I've talked about Heavenly rewards or crowns, I've encountered people who say something like, "I don't really want any rewards or crowns—I just want my little corner in Heaven." Or someone may say, "I really don't want any reward at all—just being there will be my reward."

Do you want to stand before Jesus empty-handed while everyone else is casting their crowns before Him? That attitude can sometimes be a cover-up for spiritual laziness.

I don't know about you, but I want to serve the Lord so diligently and faithfully that they have to bring a dump truck of crowns to lay at Jesus' feet so I can say, "Here, Jesus, this is all for your glory and your glory alone!" Opportunities to serve God yesterday are gone, but you have the rest of today and the rest of your life to serve Him. That way when you stand before Him you can cast your crowns at his feet and hear Him say, "Well done, good and faithful servant!"

Travel Preview

ALICE I.

⭐⭐⭐⭐⭐

I look forward to the worship! I wonder what the Heavenly choirs will sound like—everyone overwhelmed with the Spirit of God. I can't wait to sing in that group!

Will I have a chance to serve in Heaven?

We'll worship in Heaven, we'll receive crowns, and we'll lay them at the feet of Jesus, but we will also be busy serving the King. One of my favorite encounters in the New Testament is a story recorded in Luke 10:38-42 when Jesus visited the home of Mary and Martha. Martha was busy in the kitchen fixing lunch while Mary was sitting at the feet of Jesus listening to Him.

Martha represents people who feel most comfortable expressing their love to Jesus by doing acts of service. People who identify with Martha tend to be task-oriented and they usually make lists of things they need to do each day. While Martha sweated in the kitchen, Mary was perfectly satisfied to sit by Jesus and simply soak it all in.

When Martha complained about her sister, Jesus responded that Mary had chosen the one thing that was necessary— spending time with Him. While we are living in this place, *worship* ought to drive our *work* for Jesus. Not vice versa. But in Heaven, we will do BOTH with equal amounts of passion and diligence. We will all serve the King like Martha, and we will worship the King like Mary simultaneously.

So get ready to work! Heaven is not the end of our ministry for the Lord—it's just the beginning! The Bible says, *"No longer will there be any curse. The throne of God and of the Lamb will be in the city, and his servants will serve him"* (Revelation 22:3).

In addition to worshipping the King, and working for the

King, we will be reigning with the King. The Bible says we will help Jesus rule the Universe. The best translation of 1 Corinthians 6:2-3 literally says, *"Do you not know that the saints will govern the world? Do you not know that we are to govern angels?"* (MacArthur Study Bible) Every king must have prime ministers and governors to help in his administration.

40 Things You WON'T Find in Heaven

(32) Bullying

The term "govern angels" is an administrative term. Remember that God created angels to be His servants. While we are living on earth we are a little lower than these special beings. But in our resurrected state we will be ruling over angels, principalities, and powers.

Do you remember the story Jesus told about the man of noble birth who gave his servants money to invest? The ones who did well with their responsibilities were given new and greater responsibilities. The story is a picture of what Heaven will be like. We will use our gifts to administer the new Heaven and the new earth.

Your life will have a purpose in Heaven

You'll be working for the Lord, but you won't get weary or tired. You'll be energized and fulfilled. I think you'll be accomplishing something so amazing that you'll have a feeling of euphoria. Just imagine the way you felt when you accomplished something that you really wanted. Finishing a big project. Graduating from college. Getting that promotion.

I remember the first time I made a hole-in-one. It was number four at Hollytree Country Club in Tyler, Texas. The hole was exactly 155 yards from the tee box. I hit an eight-iron that drew toward the flag. It hit once and spun left and disappeared into the hole. I jumped up and down and then I fell to my knees on the tee box and lifted my hands and said, "Thank you, Jesus!" That was euphoria. But I made a double bogey on the next hole, so it was short lived! Picture your greatest moment and then just extend that sense of accomplishment and fulfillment out to eternity. That's what it's going to be like working in Heaven.

Guaranteeing your place in Heaven

I hope by this point in this travel guide that you're more excited than ever before about your final destination: Heaven. The final section is the most important part of planning your trip to Heaven, and you won't want to overlook a single detail.

PART 4

MAKING YOUR
RESERVATION IN HEAVEN

CHAPTER 12

THE ACCOMMODATIONS

Americans are fascinated with Heaven and Heavenly experiences. Go to any bookstore and you'll find a section of books on Heaven, although very few of them are written from the perspective of what the Bible says about Heaven. Instead many of the most popular books are about people's near-death experiences. In the past few years there have been three *New York Times* best-selling books written by people who claim to have died and gone to Heaven.

90 Minutes in Heaven is a book about a Baptist preacher from Texas named Don Piper. In 1989 Don was driving on a two-lane bridge across Lake Livingston when an 18-wheeler crashed head-on into his Ford Escort. He was pronounced dead at the scene. Ninety minutes later, while another Baptist preacher was praying over him, he was resuscitated and started telling about his experience after death.

Heaven Is for Real is the story of Todd Burpo, a pastor's son from Nebraska. In 2004 when Todd was four years old, he underwent emergency surgery and died. After he was resuscitated, he recovered and started talking about all he had seen in Heaven. He claimed to have seen Jesus and told his dad that Jesus had "markers." When his dad asked him what he meant, Todd pointed to his hands and feet.

To Heaven and Back was written by Dr. Mary Neal, an orthopedic surgeon. In 1999 she drowned while kayaking in a South American river. She also claimed to have died and come back. In her story she was escorted to Heaven by six or eight spirit beings who loved her and knew her. They led her down a beautiful pathway toward a domed structure, but then with sadness they told her she had to go back to earth because it wasn't her time to die.

40 Things You WON'T Find in Heaven

33 Guilt

I'm not casting doubt on the experiences of these three people. In fact Lazarus had been dead four days when Jesus called him back to life. I'm sure he could have written a first-person account of his experience and it would have been a *Jerusalem Times* bestseller.

All four of those people, including Lazarus, had what we often call a near-death experience. But a near-death experience could also be called a non-death experience. Lazarus eventually died again somewhere down the road, and these three people will eventually die also one day. The distinction I am making is that none were resurrected; they were all resuscitated.

There is only one Man who has ever died and been resurrected never to die again—that's Jesus. He died, but He rose from the dead and He is alive forevermore. This is why He—and His word, the Bible—remain the reigning expert authority on Heaven. There's nothing wrong with reading books about people who claimed to have visited Heaven. However, we should take note where some of the details they describe in

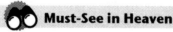

Must-See in Heaven

The Holy City

"I also saw the holy city, the new Jerusalem, coming down out of heaven from God, prepared like a bride adorned for her husband."
—REVELATION 21:2 (csb)

their accounts don't align with biblical truth. It's thrilling to think about some of the glorious things they describe, but we shouldn't let their stories guide our beliefs about Heaven. The only book that gives us an accurate portrayal of Heaven is God's Book—the Bible.

The Master Carpenter and your Heavenly home

One of the most important sections of a travel guide lists the places where travelers can stay. The choices often range from five-star resorts with a butler and luxury sheets, to simple seaside cottages to rent. If you are planning your stay in Heaven you should be interested to know about the accommodations provided.

John 14:1-4 describes this very thing: *"Do not let your hearts be troubled. Trust in God; trust also in me. In my Father's house are many rooms; if it were not so, I would have told you. I am going there to prepare a place for you. And if I go and prepare a place for you, I will come back and take you to be with me that you also may be where I am. You know the way to the place where I am going."*

Just think! For the past 2,000 years Jesus has been at His Father's House preparing your Heavenly residence. The King James Version of this passage says, *"In my Father's house are many mansions."* That's an unfortunate translation that caused some people to imagine that we're going to be living in our own mansion, separated from everyone else like in a subdivision with huge lots. Elvis even crooned about having his very own mansion just over the hilltop. But Elvis was mistaken. The actual word in Greek is *mone,* which means *rooms*. One mansion, many rooms.

But don't imagine your own private room with walls and a door you can lock like in a hotel. There will be no need for locks in Heaven. Think about sharing an enormous house with all your other Heavenly family members from every continent. It really WILL be one big, happy family. I have four grandchildren and when they are all visiting, they spread out in several rooms doing everything from artwork, playing board games, making up a play, or watching cartoons. My wife's elderly parents live in our city and they will often hang out at our house when the grandkids are present. With that many people in our house, it makes for a lot of activity and noise! I

Travel Tips

■ Don't bow down to any of the angels. They are your servants. (Hebrews 1:14)

imagine that Heaven will be a lot like having everyone "home" even though they may be doing something in another room.

What a Jewish marriage teaches about Heaven

Something I love about what Jesus says in John 14 is that He is coming for us to bring us back to the place He has prepared. The New Testament compares the return of Christ to that of a Jewish bridegroom coming to claim his bride. According to Hebrew marriage customs, there were three phases to a marriage.

First, the two fathers of the bride and groom would determine that their children were to be married. This process

 Must-See in Heaven

The Throne of God

"Immediately I was in the Spirit, and there was a throne in heaven and someone was seated on it. The one seated there had the appearance of jasper and carnelian stone. A rainbow that had the appearance of an emerald surrounded the throne. Around the throne were twenty-four thrones, and on the thrones sat twenty-four elders dressed in white clothes, with golden crowns on their heads. Flashes of lightning and rumblings and peals of thunder came from the throne. Seven fiery torches were burning before the throne, which are the seven spirits of God. Something like a sea of glass, similar to crystal, was also before the throne. Four living creatures covered with eyes in front and in back were around the throne on each side."

— REVELATION 4:2-6 (CSB)

Travel Preview

★★★★★

I am looking forward to being in the very presence of God, worshipping and enjoying Him forever, free from the presence of all sin, pain, and sorrow!

LINDA C.

necessitated talking about who would cover all the financial arrangements. For example, the groom's father would pay the dowry for the bride.

Phase two involved a betrothal. At this time the bride and groom would pledge themselves to each other. From that time on they were legally married, but they didn't yet live together as husband and wife. If you recall the Christmas story, Mary and Joseph were betrothed to each other when Mary was found to be carrying Jesus.

The betrothal stage was an extended time of great preparation. The groom would return to his father's house and start building some additional rooms to house his new family. In some areas of the Middle East today these customs are still followed. When a son is getting ready to be married, the family adds another story to their house for a place for the couple to live.

After the groom finished adding the rooms for his family, then the real fun began. In a spirit of playfulness, the groom would surprise his bride and take her away for the final stage of the wedding—the marriage celebration. This was a time of feasting, music, and dancing that would go on for several days. After this celebration, the couple would settle down in the groom's family home and live together as husband and wife.

Here's the catch. The bride wouldn't know the exact time that the groom would come to claim her. That made his arrival a surprise. She had to stay ready because he could come for her at any time. Her bridesmaids' job was to keep a lookout for the bridegroom's approach so that he would not catch the bride unaware.

Does this sound familiar? This custom is the background for the story Jesus told in Matthew 25 about the 10 bridesmaids. In that story the bridegroom waited until midnight to come and claim his bride.

This wonderful wedding custom gives us some deeper insight into our own salvation. First, consider the dowry paid for the bride. Our Heavenly Father arranged the price to pay for our salvation before the foundation of the world—offering Jesus as the Lamb of God. Second, God compares the Church to the Bride of Christ. In 2 Corinthians 11:2 Paul wrote, *"I am jealous for you with a godly jealousy I promised you to one husband, to Christ, so that I might present you as a pure virgin to him."* Since Jesus has returned to His Father's House, we are already "betrothed" to Christ. We have pledged our love and allegiance to Him. But one day He will return for His bride (Christians). He will take us to His Father's House and we will participate in the Marriage Supper of the Lamb described in Revelation 19:6-9. Like the Jewish bride we don't know the exact day or the hour when our Bridegroom will return for us. So we need to stay prepared!

Are we too Heavenly minded?

Skeptics often criticize believers because they claim that we are so obsessed with what our home in Heaven will be like that we miss out on enjoying life in the here and now. They think that all Christians talk about is "pie in the sky, by and by." I disagree. The Christian life is so much more than just going to Heaven when you die. It's not just "pie in the sky, by and by." It's also "steak on your plate while you wait."

I'd be a Christian even if we didn't go to Heaven when we die because it makes life make sense (not to mention more pleasant) here on earth. Following Christ means that we treat others with kindness and compassion. We forgive other people. We give generously to those in need. We live passionately because we know the Author of Life itself. If every person on the planet lived according to the Bible, this world would be a much better place even if there were no life beyond.

I've actually never met a believer who was "so Heavenly minded" that they there were "of no earthly good." But I've met plenty of professing Christians who are so earthly minded that they are of no Heavenly good.

C. S. Lewis once wrote in *The Joyful Christian*, **"Throughout history, the Christians who did most for this present world were those who thought most of the next...Early Christians left their mark on earth precisely because their minds were preoccupied with heaven. It is since Christians ceased thinking of the other world that we have become so ineffective in this one. Aim at heaven and you'll get the earth thrown in. Aim at the earth and you'll miss both."**

Have you made your reservation yet?

Jesus is preparing a place for you in Heaven and you will love the accommodations. But I have to ask you, "Have you confirmed your reservation?" Smart travelers always make reservations before they travel. You wouldn't just show up at the airport without a reservation and try to get on a flight.

Travel Preview

★★★★★

I picture a "line" of people waiting to greet me with JESUS in front, arms wide open with a welcoming smile on His face. Behind him will be my mother, holding my little Amy whom I lost at childbirth and she will be PERFECT. (But my brother Gary will be trying to get in front of my Mother because they always teased about who would get to Heaven first.)

GAYLA N.

There's a good chance that all the flights to your destination will be already overbooked. Although you might get a room in a hotel without a reservation, you would be much wiser to make a reservation in advance. As you'll see in the next chapter, the same is true about making a reservation for Heaven.

THE RESERVATION SYSTEM

A few years ago I discovered that there is an online service called "Reserve a Spot in Heaven." Out of curiosity I visited their website and was surprised to discover that this organization isn't in any way religious—there's nothing on their site about God or the Bible. But they offer you a money-back guarantee that you'll have a spot in Heaven. (How are you going to file a complaint with them if you don't make it?) According to the website, for a small fee you get a letter confirming your reservation in Heaven. (I'm not sure what zip code it comes from!) You also get a certificate suitable for framing with your name on it, some bogus information about Heaven and an embossed nametag for Heaven. (So God will know who you are?) Of course if you want to upgrade, for only a little more money you can get a VIP all-access pass for Heaven.

This organization also has a website to reserve a spot in hell. I am not making this up. They offer the same packages. It's clearly a spoof, but I read somewhere that thousands of people give these certificates as gag gifts every year. As P. T. Barnum said, "There's a sucker born every minute."

All kidding aside, how do you make certain that you're going to Heaven?

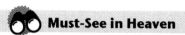 **Must-See in Heaven**

Jonah

Ask him what it was like to live in the belly of a fish for three days.

Is your name in the book?

When you are traveling somewhere and you arrive at your hotel, you walk in and approach the front desk. The first thing you do is tell them your name. Then the clerk usually checks the computer to find your reservation. If your name is there, you are assured that you'll get a room.

In the day before computers, every hotel had a reservation book where they kept a record of the names of the hotel guests. The Bible says that there are books in Heaven as well. One of them is called the Lamb's book of life. If your name is written down in His book, you have the assurance of knowing you have a place in Heaven.

Moses was the first to mention this unusual book. When he prayed for the sinful Israelites who had worshipped a golden calf, he suggested that if it would save the people, then God could blot his name out of His book. God refused that request, by the way. But somehow Moses had been made aware that God keeps an accurate record of the people who know and serve Him.

King David also wrote about God's book when he wrote the words *"all the days you ordained for me are written in your book"* (Psalm 139:16). The prophet Daniel also wrote that there would be a future judgment day when the *"books of Heaven"* are opened (Daniel 7:10).

In Luke 10 Jesus sent out 70 disciples in teams of twos. They came back rejoicing that the demons were subject to them in Jesus' name. In Luke 10:20 Jesus said, *"Do not rejoice that the spirits are subject to you, but rather rejoice that your names are written in heaven."*

Remember in the book of Revelation that the apostle John

received a vision of the new Heaven and the new earth? He describes the population of Heaven this way: *"Nothing impure will ever enter it, nor will anyone who does what is shameful or deceitful, but only those whose names are written in the Lamb's book of life"* (Revelation 21:27).

40 Things You WON'T Find in Heaven

(35) Regret

There really is a book in Heaven with the names of those who love and serve God. Trusting Christ as your Savior is the pen that writes your name there.

Can the reservation be canceled?

A few years ago I was preparing to leave for an international trip. I was scheduled to fly out of our local airport to catch a regional jet into Dallas/Ft. Worth International Airport to make the connection for my overseas flight. The plane from our local airport was delayed, and I quickly realized that I was not going to make it in time for the connection in Dallas. So I hopped in my car and started driving to DFW instead.

What I didn't realize at the time was that since I hadn't taken the first flight of my itinerary, the airline assumed I had canceled the entire trip. You guessed it. My other flights were canceled automatically! Imagine my surprise on the way to Dallas when I looked at the reservation on my phone and noticed that the flights said "canceled" in big red font. I took a deep breath and called my travel agent next. She explained what had happened, and she was able to rebook all

Travel Preview

★★★★★

Most of all I'm looking forward to my faith becoming sight and being able to walk and talk with Jesus.

KATHY B.

the flights. If I had arrived at DFW without knowing that my flights had been canceled, I might have missed the chance to rebook them. It's a scary feeling to have travel reservations canceled without your knowledge!

All the rooms in Heaven must be reserved in advance. The good news about your reservation in Heaven is that it can NEVER be canceled! Once your name is written in Heaven's book, it can never be erased. In John 10:27-30 Jesus said, *"My sheep hear my voice and I know them; and they follow me. I give them eternal life, and no man is able to pluck them out of my hands. My father is greater than me and no one is able to pluck them out of my father's hands."*

On the other hand, the Bible suggests that there are some people who expect to have a reservation in Heaven, but they will be very disappointed to discover their name is not in Heaven's reservation book. In Matthew 7:21-23 Jesus said, *"Not everyone who says to me, 'Lord Lord' will enter the kingdom of heaven, but only the one who does the will of my Father in heaven. On that day many will say to me, 'Lord, Lord, didn't we prophesy in your name, drive out demons in your name, and do many miracles in your name?' Then I will announce to them, 'I never knew you. Depart from me, you lawbreakers.'"*

These are obviously religious people who performed religious acts. But the one thing they missed was a personal relationship with Jesus. He said, "I never KNEW you." Christianity isn't a religion, it is having a personal relationship with Jesus. Do you know Him?

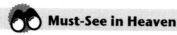 **Must-See in Heaven**

The Glorified Christ

"...and from Jesus Christ, the faithful witness, the firstborn from the dead and the ruler of the kings of the earth."
— REVELATION 1:5 (CSB)

Alternate destination

Travel Tips

■ Remember to give the people you love directions to Heaven before you leave. (John 3:16)

In this travel guide I haven't talked much about the alternative eternal destination—hell. It's not my favorite subject and I take no delight in thinking that people will be there. But the Bible makes it clear that not everyone will be in Heaven. The Bible says, *"It is appointed to man once to die; and after that the judgment"* (Hebrews 9:27). In Revelation 20 we read about a final judgment of those who rejected God's free gift of eternal life. Revelation 20:15 says, *"And anyone not found written in the Book of Life was cast into the lake of fire."*

Remember the parable in Luke 16 about the rich man suffering in Hades while Lazarus is in Paradise with God? The rich man asked Abraham (who was near Lazarus) to help him because of his torment. In response to the rich man's request, Abraham essentially said, "No way. There is a great chasm between us so that those who are here can't go to where you are (why would they want to?) and so that those who are where you are can't come here (they would ALL want to)." The rich man's next request was unusual because possibly for the first time in his life he thought about others because he realized it was too late for him. He said, "Then please send Lazarus to my house to warn my five brothers NOT to come to this place!"

There is a hell, but God is so kind and loving that He doesn't want anyone to travel there. In 2 Peter 3:9 we read, *"God is not willing that any should perish; but that all should come to repentance."* There are people who say, "I can't believe a loving God would send anyone to hell—especially those who have never heard the Gospel." It is very important to realize that God doesn't send anyone to hell. That's what free will is all about. God will not stop people from choosing hell over Heaven. They choose hell by their own free will by refusing to accept God's free gift of eternal life. In order for a person to spend eternity in hell, they must reject the love that God demonstrated on the cross. It is as Bible scholar Michael Green wrote: **"The love of God, with arms extended on a cross, bars the way to hell. But if that love is ignored, rejected, and finally refused, there comes a time when love can only weep while man pushes past into the self-chosen alienation which Christ went to the cross to avert."**

40 Things You WON'T Find in Heaven

(36) Sin

There is a reservation book in Heaven called the Lamb's Book of Life. Is your name written there? If so, then rejoice. If not, then make it the one purpose of your life to turn from your sins and place your faith in Christ—someone who loves you more than you can imagine and went to the cross because He could not bear to be apart from you.

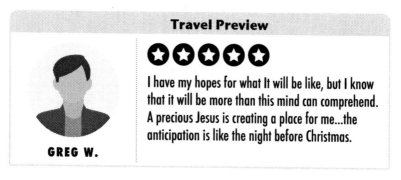

Travel Preview

I have my hopes for what It will be like, but I know that it will be more than this mind can comprehend. A precious Jesus is creating a place for me...the anticipation is like the night before Christmas.

GREG W.

Ignorance is not bliss

I've heard people say many untrue things about Heaven over the years, but one of the most perplexing things have to do with the confirmation process of making your reservation in Heaven. "Well, nobody can know for CERTAIN that you're going to Heaven when you die." Wrong. "You'll just have to wait until you die to see if you were good enough to go to Heaven." Not true. The Bible says that we CAN know for certain. In his first epistle John wrote, *"I've written these things to you who believe in the name of the Son of God that you may*

KNOW that you have eternal life" (1 John 5:13). Coming up, we'll walk through the reservation confirmation process in Heaven. Warning: the information contained in this next chapter could change your life forever.

CHAPTER 14

THE CONFIRMATION PROCESS

Some of the sweetest people I know, people whom I believe have been Christians for most of their lives, have told me they wake up in the night wondering if in the end God will not let them into Heaven because of something they've done or not done. That's not grace. That's still trying to earn it. That kind of thinking has a lot more to do with false religions than the Gospel of grace that Jesus taught.

If you are a Christian and you struggle with assurance that you're saved and going to Heaven when you die, something is wrong. Either you aren't grounded in the truth about salvation, or you've become a victim of the devil's lies. One of his lies is to keep people from being saved by convincing them that salvation has to be earned. If he cannot do that, his other great lie is to convince saved people that they must work to keep it or they'll lose it. I call that the lie of legalism compared to the Gospel of grace.

Every pastor knows that some of the people who come to church every Sunday are there relying much more on themselves to get to Heaven than they are relying on grace. They are hoping God counts attendance when they walk in the church doors. They desperately want their good deeds to outweigh their bad so they can have a shot at Heaven one day.

God's Word says in Romans 10:9, *"If you confess with your*

mouth, *'Jesus is Lord,' and believe in your heart that God has raised him from the dead, you will be saved."* Period. End of argument. If you have placed your eternal trust in Jesus, and your answer is still "I don't know" when someone asks you where you will go after you die, then I have good news for you. God wants you to move to a place of confidence and assurance—not confidence or assurance in yourself, but in God's Word. Just this once, let go of doubt and stand on the rock-solid Word of God and come to full assurance of your salvation. Then you can say by faith, "I will be with Jesus in Heaven."

Why is this assurance so important? Because if you're never sure you're saved, how are you going to witness to others? How will you tell others how to get to Heaven if you're not sure yourself? Doubt will leave you immobilized and ineffective in your faith—which is exactly where the devil wants you.

Travel Preview

★★★★★

I am looking forward to seeing Jesus and falling on my knees to worship him. Then I want to see my mother, grandmother, and aunt, give them big hugs, and talk and talk and talk!

ANNETTE L.

Three ways to know you're saved

In 1 John, John gives three points of assurance that we can look for to know that we are truly Heaven-bound. The first mark of being a Heaven-bound believer is that you will have a desire to obey God. The Bible says, *"We know that we have come to know him if we keep his commands. Whoever says, 'I know him,' but does not do what he commands is a liar, and the truth is not in that person"* (1 John 2:3-4). That doesn't mean that you will obey every command of God all the time. Nobody did that except Jesus. But a way to be certain you are Heaven-bound is if you have a sincere desire to obey the Lord.

40 Things You WON'T Find in Heaven

㊲ Boredom

The second point of assurance is that we will hate sin. The Bible says, *"No one who is born of God will continue to sin, because God's seed remains in them; they cannot go on sinning, because they have been born of God"* (1 John 3:9). This doesn't mean that you have to be sinless to enter Heaven—but you will want to sin less as you grow spiritually over time. A true believer will hate sin and will seek to live a pure life.

The third point of assurance is that we will love other believers. The Bible says, *"Dear friends, let us love one another, for love comes from God. Everyone who loves has been born of God and knows God. Whoever does not love does not know God, because God is love"* (1 John 4:7-8). Because we possess God's love, we will want to share that love with one another. The main mark Jesus gave for proof of our belief was our love. He said, *"By this everyone will know that you are my disciples, if you love one another"* (John 13:35).

The confirmation code for Heaven

Today, when you make a travel reservation, you usually receive a confirmation number. I always copy the confirmation number into my iPhone; it's my assurance that I have made the reservation. In the same way, you can have absolute assurance (confirmation) that you will be making the trip to Heaven when you die. The confirmation code is—are you writing this down?

JN316

JN316 stands for a verse in scripture, John 3:16, that has been called a summary of the entire Bible in just a few words. It is a personal promise to you, so you can add your name in the place where it says, "the world."

"For God so loved [your name] that he gave his one and only Son that whoever believes in him shall not perish but have eternal life" (John 3:16).

One of the most familiar chapters in the Bible is the 23rd Psalm. David starts by saying, *"The Lord is my Shepherd, I shall not want."* We often put so much focus on the beginning of that chapter that we miss how he concludes. He says, *"Surely your goodness and love will follow me all the days of my life, and I will dwell in the house of the Lord forever"* (Psalm 23:6). David didn't say, "I HOPE I dwell in the house of the Lord forever." He didn't say, "I MIGHT dwell in the house of the Lord forever." He said, "I WILL dwell in the house of the Lord forever." He was certain that he would spend eternity in Heaven.

Since I was a child I can remember singing a wonderful hymn about assurance. The chorus said, **"For I know whom I have believed; and am persuaded that He is able: To keep that which I've committed unto Him against that day."** It's based on the scripture found in 2 Timothy 1:12. The confirmation of our salvation is not based on our ability to keep all the commands of God; it is based on God's ability to keep us. It's one thing to be saved. But it's better to be saved and KNOW that you're saved.

They never opened the door

I read a true story about a honeymoon couple spending their first night at a nice hotel near the church where they married.

 Must-See in Heaven

Heaven's Main Street of Transparent Gold

"The twelve gates are twelve pearls; each individual gate was made of a single pearl. The main street of the city was pure gold, transparent as glass." — **REVELATION 21:21 (CSB)**

Travel Preview

PHIL B.

⭐⭐⭐⭐⭐

There are roughly 16 million colors in our world, but I believe in Heaven there are so many colors we don't have words to describe. We can appreciate roughly 42 tonal differences in music (according to Wikipedia), but how many are there in Heaven?! Just as foreign as all that sounds to us, I believe that the instant we arrive, it will not matter. We will have one activity and that is glorifying and praising our Savior. Nothing else will even come to our minds!

Early the next morning they were going to catch a flight to Hawaii for the rest of their honeymoon. The manager of the hotel was a friend of the groom's family, so he offered to take care of their room that night at no cost.

The newlyweds arrived in their special room, but they were disappointed. They had been hoping for a large suite. But instead it was a small room with only a pullout sofa bed. The bathroom didn't have a tub or a shower. The only food available was the expensive snacks in the minibar. But they didn't want to complain because it was free.

The next morning, when they checked out the manager met them and asked, "How did you enjoy your suite?" The groom smiled weakly and said, "Someone must have given us the wrong room because we had to stay in a small room and sleep on a pullout sofa."

The manager was aghast and looked again at their room number. He said, "Oh no. That was just the small den of your larger suite. Did you walk through the door into the living room and master bedroom? I had prepared a meal for you including champagne and there was an oversized tub for two! Our housekeeping staff had even sprinkled rose petals on the king-size bed. Did you not see that?"

The husband and wife sheepishly admitted that they saw

the door, but they thought it went to a closet. They never opened it. They had missed out on the wonderful honeymoon suite because they didn't open the door.

Travel Tips

■ Be sure you're "packed and ready to go" at any time. (Luke 12:20)

When I read that story I thought about how that's a parable about Heaven. Jesus loves you and has prepared an amazing room for you to enjoy for eternity. By faith, you must simply open the door. Jesus is that door because He said in John 10:9, *"I am the door. If anyone enters through me he will be saved."*

Something no one wants to talk about

A few years ago I found myself on a flight back from Houston to Tyler. I sat next to a young man who looked to be in his mid-40s. He worked in the oil and gas industry. He was a talkative guy and he was letting a few profanity bombs drop. Then he said, "What do you do?" I said, "I'm a pastor in Tyler." Without thinking he said, "*Blank,* man, I've never met a pastor before!"

He wasn't trying to be rude; he was being honest. He was just one of those rare East Texas individuals who had never set foot in a church except for a couple of weddings and funerals. Over the short trip from Houston we engaged in a friendly discussion on a variety of topics and, as sometimes happens when people find out I am a pastor, we talked about God and the Bible.

He didn't believe in God. He said, "I don't believe the Bible. I think it's just bunch of tales written by some drunk guys." As we talked it was obvious that he was a long way from even considering the possibility in believing in Jesus. But I was interested to hear what he had to say because, as you can imagine, I don't get a chance to rub elbows with guys like that very often.

Just before we landed I said, "So, tell me. What do you think is going to happen to you when you die?" He thought about it for a minute and said, "I think death is the end." Then he paused. "But I try not to think about that very much." When we got off the plane he introduced me to his girlfriend who was there to pick him up. I invited both of them to worship sometime at our church but I'm not sure if they ever did.

This man had a quick answer to everything I asked him. But the one topic he didn't want to think about was death—and what happens after death. For a person who doesn't have faith, death can be a scary and ominous thought.

In Greek mythology the edge of the world was the Strait of Gibraltar at the western edge of the Mediterranean Sea. According to the Greeks a huge statue of Hercules blocked the exit out to the Atlantic Ocean. It was called the Pillars of Hercules and it had three Latin words on it—Non Plus Ultra. Which means, "no more beyond." For centuries the sea captains believed that was the edge of the world so they never ventured far past that point.

But we know they were wrong in this estimation. Explorers like Christopher Columbus bravely went beyond the point of where they believed there was "no more beyond." In the city of Valladolid, Spain, where Columbus is buried, there's a huge monument built to his memory. Below his name we can read those three words again, "non plus ultra" or "no more beyond." But when you look closer you see that there is a lion in the monument who is tearing away at the "non." Columbus had the courage of a lion to venture beyond the point where most people thought there was "no more beyond." He discovered that there IS more beyond.

40 Things You WON'T Find in Heaven

(38) Loneliness

Like my friend on the plane, there are some people who still feel the same way about the grave. They think there is non plus ultra—no more beyond. But there was a man named Jesus who was crucified and buried. After three days He emerged from the grave as the victorious Lion of the Tribe of Judah! He clawed away the idea that there is "no more beyond" the grave and tore the doubts and fears that we might have about death and the afterlife.

He came out of that tomb—whole and alive once more—to declare to the world that there is PLUS ULTRA! There is MORE BEYOND the grave! And for those of us who know Jesus as our Savior that MORE BEYOND means spending eternity with Him in Heaven in a far, far better place. How much better? Read on.

 Must-See in Heaven

Mary

Ask her to tell you about the time Jesus turned water into wine.

CHAPTER 15

A FAR BETTER PLACE

When I was a boy my dad was a forester for International Paper Company in South Alabama. They had an office and warehouse where they kept all their heavy equipment. But they also kept a stable of five or six horses because there were some parts of the woods so thick that the only way to get through was on horseback.

On some weekends Dad would let me go out there with him to ride those horses. I remember how the horses were so reluctant to be saddled and resisted my father as he slipped bridles over their heads. When we rode away from the stable, they were stubborn and had to be urged to move.

But without fail whenever we turned back toward the stable it was a different story. We didn't have to urge them on; they would run faster than the wind, as they instinctively knew they were heading home—which is where they wanted to be all along.

We're the same way. There is something within us longing for our Heavenly home, no matter how good we may have it here on earth for a time. Many critics of Christianity dismiss our belief in a wonderful afterlife as just another fairy tale. In *Snow White*, *Cinderella*, and *Sleeping Beauty*, the prince and the princess marry and live happily ever after. "Yeah, yeah, yeah," the critics say. But have you ever wondered why so many fairy tales and legends often have plots with happy endings? I believe it's because the Bible teaches that God has *"placed eternity"* in the hearts of all people (Ecclesiastes 3:11).

In other words, God has built into our human DNA an innate longing to live happily ever after. Why else would we have this instinctive desire to live forever? In fact that intrinsic longing in our hearts is just another proof that Heaven exits and we were made for it, as much as it was made for us. The theologian J. I. Packer wrote in *Your Father Loves You*, **"As I get older, I find that I appreciate God and people and good and lovely things more and more intensely; so it is pure delight to think that this enjoyment will continue and increase in some form, literally forever. In fact, Christians inherit the destiny which fairy tales envisaged in fancy: we live and live happily, and by God's endless mercy will live happily ever after."**

God's children are homesick for Heaven

Like many of you, when I'm in a foreign country I keep my American passport handy. I enjoy experiencing a different culture, different food, and even a different language. But in the back of my mind I know that I'm not home. I have a sense that my real home is back in the country stamped on the cover of my passport: the good ol' U.S.A.

That's true of us as well. Paul wrote, *"But our citizenship is in heaven"* (Philippians 3:20).

The heroes of faith throughout the ages never felt completely at home in this world either. The Bible says the saints of old

Travel Preview

⭐⭐⭐⭐⭐

I am looking forward to seeing the glory of God for myself and understanding how the tri-unity of God works! A mystery unveiled!

BRENDA L.

"admitted that they were aliens and strangers on earth" (Hebrews 11:13). I was in line at the grocery store the other day and saw a tabloid headline that read, "There Are Aliens among Us!" I opened the magazine and read the first part of

40 Things You WON'T Find in Heaven

㊴ Doubt

the article written by some pseudoscientist talking about extraterrestrial beings. He said, "**They look and dress just like your average human being. They come in both male and female bodies. They come in all races. Some are short and skinny, and some are tall and heavy. You never know when you will encounter an alien; they could be sitting right next to you.**" I glanced around at the people standing near me as I put the magazine back. They looked just as described!

The truth is that there are aliens among us—those who follow Christ are the aliens. Peter wrote, *"I urge you as strangers and aliens in the world to abstain from sinful desires that war against your soul"* (1 Peter 2:11). But the sad truth is that many who claim to be Christians are desperately trying to feel at home here. They keep up with the Joneses buying cars and homes they cannot afford and jockey for position in society to impress people they don't even like. They've become so tightly tied to this world that the thought of going to Heaven doesn't really interest them any more.

A pastor once visited a class of elementary students and he asked, "How many of you want to go to Heaven?" All the kids except one raised their hands. The preacher said, "Son, you don't want to go to Heaven?" He said, "Yes sir. I just thought you were getting up a load to go now."

Let's be honest. Even those of us who desire to go to Heaven are not necessarily overjoyed by the idea of going right now. We say we are excited about Heaven, but we wouldn't want to answer that question while hooked up to lie detector. We have grandchildren to play with, important work that we feel must be done, two weeks at a timeshare reserved, and an upcoming community service banquet, not to mention a never-ending Netflix queue. But Heaven isn't just some add-on to a full life. If you understand what Heaven really is, you'll know it's the one place you were designed to live for eternity. God designed you for a far, far better place.

A far better place

The BEST trip you'll ever make can be your last one—to Heaven. The Bible calls it a better place. In Hebrews 11:16 the writer describes how the heroes of faith could live during times of difficulty. It's because *"they were longing for a better country—a heavenly one. Therefore God is not ashamed to be called their God, for he has prepared a city for them."*

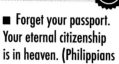

Travel Tips

■ Forget your passport. Your eternal citizenship is in heaven. (Philippians 3:20)

When Paul was writing to the church in Philippi he said, *"For to me, to live is Christ and to die is gain...I am torn between the two: I desire to depart and be with Christ, which is better by far; but it is more necessary for you that I remain in the body"* (Philippians 1:21; 23-24).

Paul used a triple superlative to describe the departure of our soul and spirit to be with Jesus. "Better by far" doesn't capture the emphasis of what he was saying; it should be translated, "Much, much, much more better." That's not good grammar, but it's good theology. Paul wasn't morbid or suicidal. He was willing to hang around gladly until God called him home, but he admitted that being with Jesus in Heaven is FAR BETTER.

So, what's so much better about Heaven? I could list hundreds of examples, but they would all fall under one of seven categories. Think of these as "Pastor David's Travel Guide to Heaven, The Summary"! Read over them anytime you need some encouragement about the wonderful eternal destination awaiting you.

SEVEN BETTER THINGS ABOUT HEAVEN

1. FAR BETTER GOVERNMENT! Don't you tire of all the talk about partisan politics? The word *politics* comes from two words—*poly* meaning "many" and *tics*, meaning "blood-sucking pests." There are all different kinds of governments in the world, from the crazy dictatorship in North Korea, to a monarchy, to a democratically elected republic. But none of these systems of government are perfect—because they are led by imperfect people. The government in Heaven is simple—it's a benevolent monarchy. There will be no political debates or differences. Everyone will love and serve the King. No CNN or Fox News needed!

2. FAR BETTER HOUSING! You may live in a mansion now, but it's not your permanent home. Every house you live in here is like a cheap run-down hotel compared to your home in Heaven. According to Google the largest residence in the world belongs to the Sultan of Brunei. It has more than two million square feet and includes 257 bathrooms and a 110-car garage. The cost of the home is about $1.4 billion. But the Father's House is FAR BETTER than any place on planet earth.

3. FAR BETTER RELATIONSHIPS! If you use social media you may have virtual friends or people who follow you. In Heaven relationships will be the exact opposite of virtual—they will be more real than you thought possible. There will be no lying, sarcasm, complaining, or manipulation. Your primary relationship will be with Jesus, and every relationship you have here with believers will be deepened and enhanced in Heaven.

4. FAR BETTER BODY! You may not like your "body type" now. But in Heaven you will have a resurrection body like the body of the Lord Jesus. So if I see you in Heaven and you ask, "How do I look?" I'll say, "You look glorious!" And I'll be telling the truth. We're going to be eating in Heaven, but you'll never get fat. In Heaven the only doctor will be the Great Physician, but there won't be any medicine because there will be no pain, no sickness, no death. The body you have now and the body you will have in Heaven can't even be compared.

5. FAR BETTER MIND! You mind will never be troubled. And you'll never struggle with memory. You will KNOW even as you are KNOWN, which means that you will literally have the mind of Christ. The mind is where fear, anxiety, and despair often camps out. Can you imagine having such a clean, pure mind that you will never have a single thought that causes you to fear, worry, or sin?

6. FAR BETTER SCENERY! No spot on earth will ever come close to the beauty of Heaven. John described a city called New Jerusalem with a crystal sea and a main street of gold with the river of life flowing down either side. The street is lined with rows upon rows of the Tree of Life.

7. FAR BETTER THINGS TO DO! One thing Heaven WON'T be is boring. It will be more fun that any experience you've ever had on earth. Basically, we'll be doing three things. First, we'll be worshipping the King. Second, we'll be serving the King. Doing what? Anything He wants us to do. He will give the orders, and we'll gladly obey. Third, we will be reigning with the King, helping God in running the Universe. So get ready to worship, serve, and rule. If that sounds like a lot to do, don't worry. We will be so energized in Heaven that we will never get tired.

Must-See in Heaven

The 12 Gates in the New Jerusalem

"The city had a massive high wall, with twelve gates. Twelve angels were at the gates; the names of the twelve tribes of Israel's sons were inscribed on the gates." — REVELATION 21:12 (csb)

Sharing directions to Heaven

I had a funny experience happen a few weeks ago when we were helping lead a travel group from church in France. We were visiting the lovely town of Rouen in an older part filled with tourists. My wife had stepped inside a jewelry store to shop and since I rarely go in stores except to pay, I waited outside. I was busy using Google Maps on my phone to map out where we were. An older couple struggling with a folded tourist map came up to me and said in a loud voice in poor French, *"Pardon. S'il vous plaît, parlez vous anglais?"*

I said, "Sure I speak English."

When they pointed to their map and asked me where to find a certain area, I could tell immediately that they were American and likely from somewhere in the Northeast. Since I already had Google Maps up on my phone I said, "You just walk down to

40 Things You WON'T Find in Heaven

(40) Good-byes

that corner and turn left and you'll find it in two blocks."

They looked at each other surprised and said in a loud voice again, enunciating each word, "Thanks! Your English is REALLY good."

I smiled and said, "That's because I'm not from around here. I'm from Texas."

They smiled back and said in their Bostonian accent, "Howdy, then." And they walked off.

I learned a lesson from that encounter. Whatever happens

in this world, we should have the sense that we're not from around here. We aren't in the world just to enjoy the sights either. Our King has put us here to give people directions about how to get to Heaven. We don't need to use a Google Maps app to share with them—we have something more certain and sure and that is the Word of God.

Travel Preview

GEORGIA A.

★★★★★

I will walk the streets of gold meeting and greeting my loved ones. We will walk into God's banquet hall filled with every food, and Heavenly beings will usher us to our seats. As Jesus' presence is made known to us, we will fall on our faces and worship Him. He will announce for us to eat and enjoy. When the banquet is over we will go to the throne room...singing and worshiping Him for all eternity.